READING EXPERT

A 5-LEVEL READING COURSE for EFL Readers

READING EXPERT *5*

Series Editor	Yoo-seung Shin
Project Editors	Donghyo Kang, Seokyung Park, Mina Song, Hyobin Park, Yuna Kim
Writers	Patrick Ferraro, Elizabeth Young, Nathaniel Galletta, John Shrader, Bryce Olk
Design	Hyunah Song
Editorial Designer	In-sun Lee
Sales	Ki-young Han, Kyung-koo Lee, In-gyu Park, Cheol-gyo Jeong, Nam-jun Kim, Woo-hyun Lee
Marketers	Hye-sun Park, Kyung-jin Nam, Ji-won Lee, Yeo-jin Kim
Special Thanks to	Seung-pyo Han, Hoe-young Kim, Hey-won Nam

Copyright©2020 by NE Neungyule, Inc.

First Printing 5 January 2020

10th Printing 15 October 2023

ISBN   979-11-253-2931-2

Photo Credits

www.istockphoto.com

www.shutterstock.com

www.dreamstime.com

p.18 Nopparat Khokthong / Shutterstock.com

INTRODUCTION

Reading Expert is a five-level reading course for EFL readers, with special relevance for junior and senior high school students. They will acquire not only reading skills but also knowledge of various contemporary and academic topics.

FEATURES

Covering Current, Academic Topics: Topics ranging from real world issues to academic subjects are covered in an easy and interesting way so that junior and senior high school students can understand them. These subjects appeal to students and can hold their attention.

Expanding Knowledge: Each unit is composed of two articles under one topic heading. These articles will help students expand their knowledge of various topics, including social and academic issues.

Practicing Reading Skills: Reading comprehension checkups encourage the use of important reading skills. They can be used to evaluate and improve students' comprehension skills, such as identifying main ideas, specific details, and implied meanings.

Tackling Longer Passages: EFL junior and senior high school students often find it difficult to read long passages because they have not received much exposure to lengthy material. Interesting and well-developed passages customized for EFL students will help learners to approach longer passages with ease. Summarizing exercises will also help them understand the flow of long passages.

Test-Oriented Questions: Many comprehension checkup questions are similar to TOEFL questions. They will be a stepping stone in preparing students for English tests at school, as well as for official English language tests such as TOEFL.

LEVEL	GRADE	WORDS LIMITS	UNITS
Reading Expert 1	Low-Intermediate	230 - 270	15
Reading Expert 2	Intermediate	250 - 300	15
Reading Expert 3		270 - 330	15
Reading Expert 4	Low-Advanced	290 - 350	15
Reading Expert 5		300 - 370	15

TO THE **STUDENTS**

Why Is Reading Challenging?

It is a very challenging, sometimes painful, experience for EFL students to read English newspapers, magazines, or books. There are various reasons for this: the high level of vocabulary and sentence structure, a lack of background knowledge on the topic, and a need for certain reading skills.

Become an Expert Reader with Reading Expert!

Reading Expert is a five-level reading course that is intended to improve your reading abilities gradually. There are 4 areas of reading strategies you need to focus on to improve your reading abilities.

1. Vocabulary Skills

When you run into an unfamiliar word, try to continue reading. In many cases a couple of unfamiliar words will not prevent general understanding of a passage. If you think they are still a barrier to further reading, use context clues. If they also do not provide enough information, it will be necessary to use your Word Book or look up the "problem word" in a dictionary.

2. Paragraph Approach

A passage is a collection of paragraphs, and the main point of each paragraph is organized into the main idea of the passage. When you read a passage, try not to just focus on the meaning of each sentence: Keep asking yourself, "What is the main point of this paragraph?" Questions on the main point of a paragraph and summary exercises will help you stay focused.

3. Understanding Long Passages

Young EFL readers have often not been exposed to long passages (more than 200 words), and they may find such passages difficult to understand. Various reading skills will be needed to understand long passages: scanning, skimming, understanding the structure of the passage, etc. Reading comprehension questions and summary exercises cover these reading skills.

4. Knowledge of the Topic

Just like when you're reading in your native language, a lack of background knowledge can prevent you from understanding the topic. The Reading Expert course covers a variety of topics, including academic subjects, social issues, world culture, and more. If you are not familiar with the topic in question, try to search for relevant information in books or on the Internet.

TO THE **TEACHER**

Series Overview

Reading Expert is a five-level reading course written by EFL teachers who have years of experience in teaching EFL students. It is simple to use in a classroom and interesting enough to keep students' attention. Each level is composed of 15 units, and each unit has two readings. Each unit contains the following sections:

Before Reading

The WARM-UP QUESTION before each reading is intended to get students ready by relating the topic to their lives. You can also help students by introducing background knowledge or explaining difficult words.

Readings

There are two readings for every unit. Before having students read the text, explain to them some important reading skills, such as scanning and skimming. After reading the passage, they can listen to an MP3 audio recording. Each reading is followed by a WORD CHECK. Students can use this section to practice guessing the meanings of the key words and expressions in context. WORD FOCUS, which shows collocations, synonyms, and antonyms, is provided alongside some passages. It will familiarize students with some natural English expressions while increasing their range of English vocabulary.

Comprehension Checkups

Readings are also followed by comprehension checkup questions. These are intended to help students identify the MAIN IDEA or subject of the passage and understand DETAILS. Questions related to reading skills are sometimes included.

Summary

A SUMMARY is provided for each reading and it can take a number of different forms, such as a basic summary, a graphic organizer, a note-taking summary, etc. All of these forms are designed to improve students' ability to understand and summarize a passage. There are various ways to use this section, such as assigning it as homework or having the students complete it without referring to the reading. It tests whether students understand the text as a whole.

Word Review Test

Learning vocabulary is important for EFL readers. They need to review key words, expressions, and difficult or unfamiliar words. A WORD REVIEW TEST comes at the end of every two units and is intended to test students' vocabulary.

TABLE OF **CONTENTS**

The Carnival of Blacks and Whites may not sound like a colorful event, but it actually is! This annual festival is held in Pasto, Colombia, from January 4th through 6th and includes parades with elaborately designed floats and costumes. It is also one of the oldest carnival celebrations in South America and was officially declared part of Colombia's cultural heritage in 2002.

The festival's earliest origins can be traced back to the 17th century. After a slave rebellion in the city of Remedios in 1607, the region's slaves began to demand a special day off. In response, the king of Spain, who ruled Colombia at that time, declared January 5th a day on which all slaves could enjoy temporary freedom. ⓐ Upon hearing the news, the region's slaves celebrated with music and dancing, blackening the city's white walls with coal. ⓑ Their masters even painted their own faces black to take part in the fun. ⓒ In this way, a great tradition began. ⓓ

Sometime around the mid-19th century, this tradition was brought to Pasto, and the modern Carnival of Blacks and Whites was born. Today, it begins with a big parade on January 4th. People dress up in colorful, old-fashioned clothes and walk through the city's streets. The two main events of the carnival are held on January 5th and 6th. First is the Day of the Blacks. People of all races and ethnicities cover themselves with black paint, and orchestras give free concerts in the street. On the next day, the Day of the Whites, people throw white powder on one another. These two events symbolize equality and **integrate** all of Colombia's citizens, regardless of race or ethnicity.

The Carnival of Blacks and Whites is considered to be one of the liveliest festivals in South America, full of friendly people who welcome visitors from all across the globe. It is a time when everyone can come together to have fun. But more importantly, it is a celebration of Colombia's racial diversity and unity.

WORD FOCUS

⊜ Synonyms for

integrate

unite
blend
incorporate

Choose the correct words for the blanks from the highlighted words in the passage.

1. _____ lasting only a limited time
2. _____ in a highly creative or detailed way
3. _____ a decorated vehicle that is part of a parade or street celebration
4. _____ having qualities that are out of style or similar to sth from the past
5. _____ an attempt to change the government or leader of a country

*__sb__: somebody / __sth__: something

1 What is the best title for the passage?
   a. The Popularity of Carnivals in Colombia
   b. The Origin of the Carnival of Blacks and Whites
   c. Colombia: A Country of Racial Diversity and Unity
   d. Carnival of Blacks and Whites: Celebrating Equality and Integration

DETAILS

2 Where would the following sentence best fit in paragraph 2?

   | The next day, the slaves responded by painting their faces white. |

3 What do the two main events mean according to paragraph 3?

   _____

4 Which is closest in meaning to diversity?
   a. variety   b. equality   c. similarity   d. harmony

5 Which is NOT true about the Carnival of Blacks and Whites according to the passage?
   a. It is an annual carnival held for three days in Pasto, Colombia.
   b. It officially became part of the cultural heritage of Colombia in 2002.
   c. The modern version of the carnival started in Remedios in the 17th century.
   d. On the first day, people parade through the streets in colorful clothes.

SUMMARY

6 Use the words in the box to fill in the blanks.

   | white   parade   freedom   heritage   black   master   rebellion |

   The Carnival of Blacks and Whites takes place annually in Pasto, Colombia, from
   January 4th through 6th. The festival's origins date back to a 17th-century slave
   _____ in another city. The king of Spain responded to the rebellion by making
   January 5th a day of temporary _____ for slaves. The first day of the festival
   features a colorful _____. On the second day, people paint themselves with
   black paint, and on the third day they cover each other in _____ powder. This
   lively festival celebrates Colombia's racial diversity and unity.

The ancient Egyptians are remembered for their impressive tombs and monuments. There is, however, a less famous piece of ancient Egyptian life that is a part of every Egyptian home today. It is
5 *aish baladi,* a flatbread made from wheat. In ancient Egypt, wheat was one of the main sources of food and was considered a sacred plant of the gods. The wheat-growing tradition brought about *aish baladi,* which has remained a unique part of Egyptian culture.

Aish baladi can be found everywhere in Egypt. In Cairo, you are never far from
10 someone selling freshly baked *aish baladi.* The pieces of flatbread are round and puffed up with air in the middle. They have cracked wheat on top and come in different textures, from soft and fluffy to dry. Because they are made from whole wheat, they have the nutritional benefits of this grain's high fiber, vitamin, and mineral content. At mealtime, *aish baladi* is perfect for making sandwiches or scooping up soft food and sauces.

15 Archaeology has shown that *aish baladi* has been around for a very long time. Artwork in ancient tombs includes pictures of food that looks just like the round flatbread made today, and even preserved pieces of bread have been found. The ancient Egyptians made bread by adding wild yeast to their dough and baking the dough in ovens made from the Nile's red mud. The recipe for *aish baladi* and the **method** of baking it have
20 stayed the same for thousands of years.

The importance of bread since ancient times has influenced the Egyptian language and culture. Even the name *aish baladi* reflects this. It is much different from the typical Arabic word for "bread." It is formed from words meaning "traditional" (*baladi*) and "life" (*aish*). During the Egyptian revolution of 2011, the slogan "bread, freedom, and social
25 justice" was used because bread stands for all the basic needs of life.

Like many foods, *aish baladi* is more than just a meal. It represents generations of tradition and thousands of years of history. And as it still plays a large role in modern life, its story continues to grow.

WORD CHECK

Choose the correct words for the blanks from the highlighted words in the passage.

1. _____ being connected with a god or religion
2. _____ having the usual qualities of sth
3. _____ the feeling of sth when you touch it
4. _____ to show the nature of sth
5. _____ a building or structure that is a reminder of a person or event

Identifying cause and effect

To recognize cause and effect, we identify words or phrases such as *because*, *since*, *so that*, *as a result*, etc. We can also identify how the information fits together. Start with a *why* question to discover the cause, and then you can better understand the effect.

MAIN IDEA

1 **What is the passage mainly about?**

  a. the way Egyptian bread is prepared and baked

  b. the importance of bread to Egyptian culture

  c. the differences between Egypt and other Arab countries

  d. the influence of ancient Egypt on the modern world

DETAILS

2 **Why does the writer mention tombs and monuments in paragraph 1?**

  a. to honor their beauty and magnificence

  b. to correct misinformation about them

  c. to explain how they are related to ancient Egypt

  d. to give examples of what ancient Egypt is best known for

3 **Which is NOT mentioned about *aish baladi*?**

  a. its shape and texture

  b. its nutritional value

  c. the way its recipe was preserved

  d. the meaning of its name

4 **Write T if the statement is true or F if it's false.**

  (1) Ancient Egyptians used wheat for a large part of their diet.   _____

  (2) The recipe for *aish baladi* has changed a lot since ancient times.   _____

  (3) *Aish baladi* is a common term for "bread" in Arabic.   _____

5 **Why was the word for "bread" used in the slogan for the Egyptian revolution of 2011?**

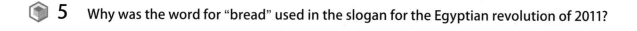

SUMMARY

6 **Match each main point to the correct paragraph in the passage.**

(1) Paragraph 1 •   • ⓐ *Aish baladi* remains very popular and has unique characteristics.

(2) Paragraph 2 •   • ⓑ The importance of *aish baladi* continues today.

(3) Paragraph 3 •   • ⓒ Artifacts show that *aish baladi* is ancient and has changed very little over time.

(4) Paragraph 4 •   • ⓓ *Aish baladi* was created because ancient Egyptians grew a lot of wheat.

(5) Paragraph 5 •   • ⓔ The language and culture of Egypt has been influenced by bread.

WARM-UP QUESTION • Do you memorize your friends' phone numbers?

Dementia is a well-known disorder that affects memory and concentration. Dementia patients often find it hard to remember simple things, such as phone numbers and people's names. While it is typically diagnosed in the elderly, there has been a recent and troubling increase in dementia-like symptoms in teenagers and adults in their 20s and 30s. This new type of dementia has been called "digital dementia."

Why do we call it "digital"? It has been blamed on the excessive use of smartphones and long hours spent in front of television and computer screens. When these devices are overused, the left side of the brain, which is responsible for logic and reasoning, tends to get overworked. _____(A)_____, the right side of the brain, which supports cognitive functions like memory, attention, and the processing of ideas, is hardly utilized. This imbalance in how the brain is used leads to memory problems. Because of this, experts in some countries have recommended banning smartphones and other electronic devices from classrooms.

_____(B)_____, people these days tend to store phone numbers and other bits of information on their smartphones instead of in their **mind**s. It has been suggested that the resulting lack of mental stimulation hinders memory and brain development. This idea is supported by the fact that in South Korea, where over 90% of teenagers own a smartphone, there has been an alarming increase in cases of digital dementia.

So what can you do to fight digital dementia? First, try to use digital devices only when you need to. Also, memorizing phone numbers of family members and friends is a good way to keep your memory sharp. Reading books and keeping a diary are great activities for keeping the brain stimulated, too. Finally, aerobic exercise enhances blood circulation in the brain and is good for your mental health. These activities can help you lead a healthy life and avoid becoming a victim of digital dementia.

Choose the correct words for the blanks from the highlighted words in the passage.

1. _____ being related to thinking
2. _____ to keep sb or sth from starting, doing, or completing an activity
3. _____ causing worry or upset feelings
4. _____ being more than what is generally considered acceptable
5. _____ to identify an illness

Skimming

Skimming is looking quickly through the text to get a general idea of what it is about. We move our eyes quickly through the whole text, allowing us to identify the purpose of the passage or the main idea.

MAIN IDEA

1 **What is the best title for the passage?**

a. What Causes Digital Dementia

b. Banning Digital Devices from Classrooms

c. The Growing Problem of Digital Dementia

d. The Consequences of Smartphone Addiction

DETAILS

2 **What happens to the left side of the brain when digital devices are overused?**

_____

3 **What is the best pair for blanks (A) and (B)?**

	(A)	(B)
a.	On the other hand	However
b.	Similarly	Furthermore
c.	Besides	Otherwise
d.	Meanwhile	In addition

4 **Which is closest in meaning to <u>sharp</u>?**

a. intense   b. plain   c. alert   d. extreme

5 **Which of the following is NOT true according to the passage?**

a. Digital dementia is increasingly diagnosed in teenagers and young adults these days.

b. The excessive use of digital devices causes the two sides of the brain to be disconnected.

c. Lack of mental stimulation makes it difficult for the brain to develop.

d. It is helpful to read books or keep a diary to prevent digital dementia.

SUMMARY

6 Use the words in the box to fill in the blanks.

imbalance	logical	keep	mental	exercising	memorize	overuse

Digital Dementia

Definition	• a memory condition caused by the _____ of electronic devices
Causes and Effects	• using electronic devices too much → _____ in the brain's processing → memory problems • storing information on digital devices → shortage of _____ stimulation → hindrance to brain development
Solutions	• Don't use digital devices when it's not necessary. • _____ the phone numbers of people in your life. • Read books and keep a diary. • Maintain your brain health by _____.

WARM-UP QUESTION • Which do you prefer, Western medicine or Chinese medicine?

Sometimes, two people can look at the same problem and come up with two very different methods for solving it. Such is the case with practitioners of Western medicine and those of Chinese, or Oriental, medicine. Our reporter sat down with two physicians to learn more
5 about what sets them apart.

Reporter: Dr. Smith, explain for us the general approach that Western physicians take toward medicine.

Dr. Smith: Modern medicine evolved around
10 the same time as the other physical sciences. Because we view it as a science, our medical understanding is guided by carefully designed laboratory experiments. Likewise, the treatments we develop often come from the
15 laboratory in the form of chemically synthesized drugs.

Reporter: Dr. Wu, how does Chinese medicine differ from what Dr. Smith just described?

Dr. Wu: If Western medicine is a science,
20 Chinese medicine can be thought of as an art. Just as art is based on cultural tradition and evolves through the centuries, so does our practice of medicine. _____(A)_____, Chinese treatments typically utilize the careful
25 administration of pure, natural herbs rather than synthesized drugs.

Reporter: Dr. Smith, what is one drawback of the Western approach to medicine?

Dr. Smith: Unfortunately, we view the human body as a machine, and it follows that each 30 illness is seen as a defect in the machine. Repair or replace the defective part, and the machine should function normally. _____(B)_____, because the human body is a complex set of systems linked with one another, the true 35 nature of how it works as a whole is not fully understood yet.

Reporter: Dr. Wu, what about a weakness in the Chinese approach?

Dr. Wu: I don't think we put enough emphasis 40 on studying and investigating the causes of specific illnesses. Western doctors have powerful diagnostic tools at their disposal, something that many Chinese doctors either lack or simply aren't interested in. 45

Reporter: What are your predictions for the future of medicine?

Dr. Wu: I believe both traditions will work together more closely in the future. Both have important innovations to offer, and in 50 combination they could be quite effective.

Dr. Smith: Yes, I agree.

WORD CHECK

Choose the correct words for the blanks from the highlighted words in the passage.

1. _____ to make use of sth
2. _____ stress put on sth to show its importance
3. _____ a person who works in a certain field
4. _____ an imperfection in a system or a machine
5. _____ a new idea or way of doing sth

READING SKILL

Identifying contrasts
To better understand a passage, it is helpful to identify contrasting examples. Certain words will give you clues about when the writer is contrasting information. Look for words like *but*, *although*, *whereas*, *yet*, and *however*, and phrases like *on the other hand*.

MAIN IDEA

1 What is the interview mainly about?

   a. the history of modern medicine in the West
   b. the differences between Western and Chinese medicine
   c. the serious side effects of chemically synthesized drugs
   d. the popularity of Chinese medicine in Western countries

DETAILS

2 According to Dr. Smith, Western medicine largely relies on laboratory experiments because _____.

   a. it is a healing art rather than a pure science
   b. synthesized drugs should be carefully administered
   c. medicine is regarded as a branch of science in the West
   d. Westerners don't know how to use herbs for treatments

3 What is the best pair for blanks (A) and (B)?

	(A)	(B)
a.	Likewise	Instead
b.	Moreover	However
c.	Therefore	In other words
d.	Yet	Meanwhile

4 Which of the following is NOT true according to the passage?

   a. Western medicine relies on the use of synthesized drugs for treatments.
   b. Herbs are used as treatments in Chinese medicine.
   c. Western medicine doesn't fully understand how the human body works as a whole.
   d. Chinese medicine has abundant tools to diagnose diseases.

SUMMARY

5 Use the words in the box to fill in the blanks.

| defective | science | herbs | culture | diagnostic | evolve | machine |

Western vs. Chinese medicine

General approach	Drawbacks	Future
• Western medicine is a (1)_____, with synthetic drugs. • Chinese medicine is an art, with (2)_____ used in treatments.	• Western medicine sees the body as a (3)_____. • Chinese medicine is not focused on (4)_____ investigation.	• Both traditions might be used side by side.

15

WORD REVIEW TEST

[1~3] Choose the word that is closest in meaning to the underlined word.

1. The article explains the <u>origins</u> of the tradition.
   a. events   b. roots   c. features   d. purposes

2. We should try to preserve our national <u>heritage</u>.
   a. tribe   b. security   c. reputation   d. legacy

3. The temple is considered a <u>sacred</u> place.
   a. safe   b. holy   c. beautiful   d. beneficial

[4~7] Connect the matching words in columns A and B.

A	B
4. take •	• a. in new clothes
5. declare •	• b. part in a competition
6. dress up •	• c. the way people behave
7. influence •	• d. a state of emergency

[8~11] Choose the best word to complete each sentence.

8. We're finding better ways to _____ refugees into our society.
   a. integrate   b. punish   c. modify   d. symbolize

9. The changes in the rules _____ public opinion.
   a. reflected   b. decorated   c. participated   d. behaved

10. The fabric has a soft _____.
    a. tomb   b. tradition   c. texture   d. recipe

11. *ASAP* _____ "as soon as possible."
    a. puts up   b. brings about   c. stands for   d. celebrates with

[12~15] Choose the correct word for each definition.

unity   coal   respond   remain   method   ethnicity

12. the condition of being together and in agreement:

13. a way of doing something:

14. to react to the actions of another:

15. a hard, black substance dug up from the ground:

[1~4] Choose the word that is closest in meaning to the underlined word.

1. The biggest <u>drawback</u> of this type of laptop is the screen size.
    a. strength   b. innovation   c. function   d. disadvantage

2. We developed new technology to <u>utilize</u> our resources effectively.
    a. get   b. use   c. export   d. store

3. People with a <u>disorder</u> must be given proper attention.
    a. process   b. experiment   c. exhaustion   d. illness

4. She was a <u>victim</u> of bullying and false rumors at her school.
    a. supporter   b. survivor   c. sufferer   d. attacker

[5~8] Connect the matching words in columns A and B.

A	B
5. differ •	• a. normally
6. function •	• b. from family to family
7. ban •	• c. to prefer new items
8. tend •	• d. drinking and driving

UNIT 02

[9~11] Choose the best word to complete each sentence. (Change the form if needed.)

increase   memory   replace   diagnostic   reasoning   defect

9. The mechanic examined the engine and found a serious _____.

10. It is essential to use scientific _____ to draw your conclusion.

11. The _____ test for lung cancer appears to be very accurate.

[12~16] Choose the correct word for each definition.

electronic   circulation   evolve   concentration   sharp   dementia

12. the ability to think carefully about a particular object or activity:

13. to develop into a different, often more advanced, form:

14. an illness that makes you lose the ability to think and behave normally:

15. the movement of blood around your body:

16. fully aware and attentive:

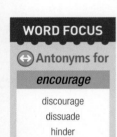

Y ou probably use a Facebook or Twitter account to keep in touch with your friends and share pictures and information from your daily life. But social media has the potential to do much more. For example, some people have started using social media to
5 give a voice to those who are less fortunate. In this way, it can be more than just a fun way to share information; it can also make a real difference in people's lives.

Internationally recognized activist Mark Horvath has been doing just that. Since starting a website in 2008, he has been sharing the stories of homeless men and women
10 across the United States and Canada. He started out by interviewing homeless people in Seattle and posting the conversations on YouTube. He was **encourage**d by the large number of views the videos got, and once he realized he had supporters, he went on a road trip and interviewed people across the United States. Then in 2010, he created another website to help homeless people get involved with social media, tell their stories,
15 and contact support services.

Horvath has said that when homeless people have a problem, no one wants to listen to them. He knows this because he was once homeless himself. He has said that, at that time, he felt more powerless than anyone could ever imagine. But now, thanks to his activism, people are listening. Many have even started to _____ (A) _____.
20 When people in Calgary saw his interview with a man named Donny, who had lived on the street for 21 years, they helped him find housing. Then after watching the videos on Horvath's website, a farmer in Arkansas donated 40 acres of land to be used to produce food for low-income families.

While social media is most often used to simply share one's opinions and ideas
25 about daily life, its possibilities are endless. Most people just think of the homeless as street people begging for money. They rarely hear or think about those people's struggles or their attempts to rebuild their lives. Horvath's work is a great example of how social media can shatter stereotypes and give a voice to those in need.

WORD CHECK

Choose the correct words for the blanks from the highlighted words in the passage.

1. _____ to ask for sth without pride
2. _____ sb who wants sb or sth to succeed
3. _____ to break or smash sth, such as glass, into small pieces
4. _____ to remain in contact with sb or sth, especially over a long time
5. _____ the pursuit of big change, especially political or social change

1 What is the best title for the passage?
a. Media's Significant Impact on Our Lives
b. Social Media: A Fun Way to Share Your Story
c. Mark Horvath's Efforts to Build Homes for the Homeless
d. How Mark Horvath Has Made a Difference with Social Media

2 Which is closest in meaning to <u>recognized</u>?
a. certified   b. known   c. trained   d. infamous

3 According to paragraph 2, why did Mark Horvath create another website in 2010?

_____

4 What is the best expression for blank (A)?
a. take action
b. depend on his help
c. make their own videos
d. interview the homeless

5 Which is NOT true about Mark Horvath according to the passage?
a. He has been posting stories of the homeless since 2008.
b. His videos have attracted lots of views on YouTube.
c. He doesn't know from experience what being homeless is like.
d. He inspired people to find a house for a homeless person.

6 Use the words in the box to fill in the blanks.

| posting | donated | inspired | struggle | share | selling | voice |

Most people just use social media to share information about their daily lives. But Mark Horvath has set a great example by using it to give a(n) _____ to the homeless. He started by interviewing homeless people and _____ the videos on YouTube. Later, he made a website to help homeless people use social media to _____ their stories. Horvath's videos have _____ many people to help those in need. Horvath's compassionate work shows how social media can make a real difference in people's lives.

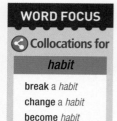

WARM-UP QUESTION • Do you know how the number of viewers of a TV program is calculated?

When discussing the success or failure of television programs, people generally refer to the number of viewers. This is an important statistic, as companies use it to make advertising decisions.
5 But have you ever wondered how this number is determined? There is actually an entire field dedicated to doing so, and it is known as audience research.

Of course, it is impossible to find out what every person in the world is watching at any particular time. Instead, a sample audience is surveyed. In America, this sample
10 consists of 25,000 households. In the past, these families were asked to keep a diary of their viewing habits and submit it once a week. Then in the 1990s, this method was abandoned in favor of TV meters. These were devices that were attached to each household's televisions in order to record exactly what the family watched.

Nowadays, however, most TV meters have been replaced with "people meters."
15 These devices can gather more detailed information. For example, they can track what each individual member of a household watches. When you sit down to watch TV, you push a personalized button that activates the people meter. You push it again when you are finished viewing. This lets advertisers know important things, such as which shows are popular with women or which age groups like a certain show best.

20 ⓐ Unfortunately, there are some doubts that these rating figures are reliable. ⓑ Collectively, the 25,000 American households used in audience research represent only about 0.02% of the total population. ⓒ Therefore, the viewing habits of 99.9% of America are being ignored. ⓓ

There is also some specific criticism of people meters. They rely on people
25 consistently pressing their buttons when they enter or exit the room. Special cameras have been created to fix this problem, but their high cost has prevented them from being installed in most households. Furthermore, people increasingly watch TV in places other than their own home, such as restaurants or other public locations. And, of course, the growing popularity of watching shows on the Internet and smartphones creates a whole
30 new problem for accurate audience research.

WORD
CHECK

Choose the correct words for the blanks from the highlighted words in the passage.

1. _____ with little variation from reality or the truth
2. _____ a number used to represent specific information
3. _____ the people living together in a house or apartment
4. _____ to place sth in a location and prepare it for use
5. _____ the people who are watching or listening to an event

1 What is the passage mainly about?

    a. the latest advances in television broadcast technology

    b. why people are turning to the Internet for entertainment

    c. the methods and limits of performing audience research

    d. various strategies to attract more viewers to television shows

DETAILS

2 In what way can TV viewers' information be gathered under the "people meter" system?

_____

3 Where would the following sentence best fit in paragraph 4?

| Part of the problem is the sample size. |

4 Which is NOT mentioned as a problem with the current audience research methods?

    a. The sample size is too small to show the exact number of viewers.

    b. When buttons are not pressed, the viewers aren't taken into consideration.

    c. Privacy concerns prevent cameras from being installed to gather detailed information.

    d. The ratings only represent people who watch TV at home.

SUMMARY

5 Use the words in the box to fill in the blanks.

sample	number	attached	Internet	recorded	diary

Audience Research

- Estimates the _____ of people watching a TV program
- Surveys a sample audience
- Has evolved over the years
  - keeping a(n) _____: viewers wrote down everything they watched
  - TV meter: _____ to each household's television to record what was watched
  - people meter: tracks which people are watching each show
- Several problems
  - too small a(n) _____ size
  - failure to turn the meters on and off
  - watching TV outside of the home or on a computer

WORD FOCUS

⊜ Synonyms for

harmful

damaging
dangerous
adverse
negative

WARM-UP QUESTION • Have you ever heard about creatures that share their lives?

No one can live life alone, but some creatures share their lives more than others. Nature's closest relationships between different species are called symbiosis. It is a name formed from the Greek words meaning "together" and "life." In the past, the term "symbiosis" was used only for relationships in which both creatures benefit. Today, however, it refers to a wider variety of interactions.

The first type of symbiosis is called mutualism, and it describes the original meaning of the word. In mutualism, both species gain something from their interaction. Clownfish and sea anemones are a good example. Clownfish live within the stinging tentacles of sea anemones. They are immune to the stings, and the tentacles give them protection from predators. In return, the clownfish eat parasites off of the anemones and lure other fish into the anemones' grasp.

The second type of symbiosis is called commensalism. In this type of interaction, one organism benefits while the other is hardly affected at all. Remoras are fish with an organ on their heads that works like a suction cup. They use this organ to attach themselves to larger sea creatures, including sharks. This is not **harmful** to the larger animal. Fish have to swim or move their gills constantly to get oxygen out of the water, but thanks to their hosts, remoras can move quickly through the water without using up their own energy.

The third type of symbiosis is called parasitism. In this case, one of the living things in the relationship benefits by harming the other. Fleas and ticks are all-too-familiar examples. Fleas live on the body of an animal and suck its blood when they get hungry. Ticks bury their head in an animal's skin, also to suck its blood. The parasites benefit by getting a constant supply of food, but their hosts suffer. Besides taking nutrients away from the host, these parasites also carry many diseases that can be deadly.

Symbiotic relationships are a fascinating example of how creatures are connected. It would be nice if mutualism and commensalism were the only forms, but parasitism is unavoidable, and it shows that organisms will find any way possible to survive.

WORD CHECK

Choose the correct words for the blanks from the highlighted words in the passage.

1. _____ capable of causing death
2. _____ protected from a disease or toxin
3. _____ an action that affects all people or things involved
4. _____ an animal that kills other animals for food
5. _____ a part of an animal's body that performs distinct functions

READING SKILL

Identifying the main idea
When you recognize the main idea of a passage, you can focus on what is important and skim over other information. It's common for an author to mention the main idea in the first paragraph and repeat it again in the conclusion.

MAIN IDEA

1 **What is the best title for the passage?**
   a. Animal Interactions: Helpful, Neutral, and Harmful
   b. Three Strategies Animals Use to Find Food
   c. Biology Terms from the Past, Present, and Future
   d. Shocking Examples of Blood-Sucking Parasites

DETAILS

2 **What did the term "symbiosis" refer to in the past?**
   _____

3 **Which is closest in meaning to lure?**
   a. force   b. transform   c. attract   d. disguise

4 **Write T if the statement is true or F if it's false.**
   (1) The current meaning of "commensalism" is the same as the original   _____
       meaning of "symbiosis."
   (2) Remoras help larger animals move quickly through the water.   _____
   (3) Both fleas and ticks are capable of giving diseases to their hosts.   _____

5 **Which of the following is NOT mentioned in the passage?**
   a. how the tentacles of sea anemones help clownfish
   b. what remoras use to attach themselves to other animals
   c. the effects that parasites have on their hosts
   d. the kinds of animals that fleas live on

SUMMARY

6 **Use the words in the box to fill in the blanks.**

| protect   steal   swim   benefit   harming   affected   survival |

Symbiosis

Mutualism	Commensalism	Parasitism
▪ Both organisms (1) _____ from the interaction. ▪ Sea anemones (2) _____ clownfish, and clownfish clean anemones.	▪ One organism benefits, and the other is hardly (3) _____. ▪ Remoras travel by attaching themselves to larger sea animals.	▪ One organism benefits by (4) _____ the other. ▪ Fleas and ticks (5) _____ nutrients from their hosts.

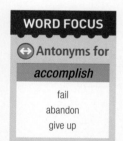

Wildfires sweep through forests and plains, burning everything in their path. Unlike animals, plants have no way of running from the flames. However, they have
5 developed several survival strategies to protect themselves from fire. In some cases, fire is even a necessary part of their life cycles.

Some plants have seeds that will only sprout after a fire. Certain pine trees grow their seeds inside of protective cones sealed up with a glue-like substance called resin.
10 When a fast-moving fire sweeps through, the resin melts and the seeds eventually fall to the ground and grow. Other plants have seeds that stay unchanged in the soil for years. The seeds have tough coatings that don't allow them to grow until they have been exposed to extreme heat or the chemical changes that a fire produces in the soil.

ⓐ A second survival strategy involves protecting the living tissues of adult plants
15 from fire. ⓑ It keeps the tree safe from intense heat even when it is surrounded by flames. ⓒ Another variation of this strategy is found in plants that grow moist tissues for protection. ⓓ During a fire, the moisture prevents them from burning or becoming dehydrated.

In other cases, the fire survival strategy is focused on keeping vulnerable parts of
20 the plant out of the reach of flames. Several types of trees **accomplish** this by growing tall trunks with branches only near the top. Some of them drop their dead lower branches as they grow, which ensures that living branches at the top will stay safe from fire. This is important since dead branches provide fuel that could keep flames burning dangerously close to the living flowers, leaves, and other important structures at the top of the tree.

25 Other fire protection strategies exist in the plant kingdom. Some eucalyptus species, for example, have buds under their bark that form new branches only after a fire, while fire lilies remain flowerless until fire causes them to quickly bloom. Fire is a part of nature, and plants have a multitude of ways to live with it.

WORD FOCUS

↔ Antonyms for

accomplish

fail
abandon
give up

WORD CHECK

Choose the correct words for the blanks from the highlighted words in the passage.

1. _____ a group of plant or animal cells
2. _____ capable of being easily harmed
3. _____ to produce buds or leaves
4. _____ very strong or extreme in degree
5. _____ to remove water from sth

24

1   What is the passage mainly about?
   a. how plants avoid being killed by fires
   b. which plants are found in hot climates
   c. what kinds of bark different trees have
   d. why fire causes tree seeds to grow

2   Where would the following sentence best fit in paragraph 3?

   > Some trees have thick bark that is very difficult to burn.

3   Which of the following is NOT true according to the passage?
   a. The seeds of certain pine trees come out of their cones after a fire.
   b. Some plants have seeds that can stay safe in the soil for a long time.
   c. The moist tissues of some plants keep them from being harmed by fire.
   d. Eucalyptus trees hide their buds beneath their bark after a fire.

4   What are the TWO ways some trees keep their vulnerable parts out of the reach of flames?

   _____

5   Which is closest in meaning to ensures?
   a. distracts   b. aids   c. ceases   d. guarantees

6   Use the words in the box to fill in the blanks.

exposed   bloom   fuel   dehydrated   unchanged   high

Plants' Strategies

Protecting seeds	▪ When a fire sweeps through, the seeds inside some pine cones fall to the ground and grow. ▪ The seeds of some plants remain _____ in the soil, and they start to grow only after they are _____ to fire.
Protecting living tissues	▪ Some trees have thick bark, which keeps them safe from heat. ▪ Some plants grow moist tissues, which keep them from burning or becoming _____.
Protecting vulnerable parts	▪ Some tall trees grow their branches _____ up to keep them above the flames. ▪ The dead lower branches fall off so that they can't be used as _____ by the fire.

WORD REVIEW TEST

[1~4] Choose the word that is closest in meaning to the underlined word.

1. The organization <u>donated</u> all the profits from the charity event to cancer research.
    a. reinforced   b. invested   c. accumulated   d. contributed

2. The student made no <u>attempt</u> to improve his poor grade.
    a. innovation   b. success   c. effort   d. decision

3. The play we saw yesterday <u>consisted of</u> three main plots.
    a. accounted for   b. focused on   c. was attached to   d. was composed of

4. Tomorrow is the final day to <u>submit</u> my philosophy paper.
    a. activate   b. expand   c. turn in   d. give away

[5~8] Connect the matching words in columns A and B.

A	B
5. interview •	• a. a big difference
6. make •	• b. your support
7. fix •	• c. candidates for the position
8. rely on •	• d. a problem

[9~12] Choose the best word to complete each sentence. (Change the form if needed.)

statistics   share   track   household   stereotype   homeless

9. I would like to go on TV to _____ my views about the issue widely.

10. The military continued to _____ the mysterious plane on their radar.

11. This electric oven is being used in over 40,000 _____.

12. According to _____, the number of drunk drivers is increasing.

[13~16] Choose the correct word for each definition.

abandon   rebuild   fortunate   media   doubt   struggle

13. to make something strong again:

14. a hard effort to get or achieve something:

15. to stop or give up:

16. all the sources of news and information:

[1~4] Choose the word that is closest in meaning to the underlined word.

1. I'm sure that he will <u>accomplish</u> the task at hand.
    a. plan　　　　　b. achieve　　　　c. approve　　　　d. revise

2. These chemicals are <u>deadly</u>, so handle them carefully.
    a. harmless　　　b. rare　　　　　c. fatal　　　　　d. positive

3. They're laughing so hard they can <u>hardly</u> breathe.
    a. incredibly　　b. extremely　　　c. scarcely　　　d. highly

4. After much consideration, she <u>eventually</u> took up my offer.
    a. desirably　　　b. happily　　　　c. greatly　　　　d. finally

[5~8] Connect the matching words in columns A and B.

A		B
5. suck •		• a. a clever strategy
6. develop •		• b. to the ground
7. fall •		• c. time and energy
8. use up •		• d. people's blood

[9~11] Choose the best word to complete each sentence.

9. We are making a new marketing _____ to increase sales.
    a. hardship　　　b. strategy　　　　c. loss　　　　　d. damage

10. Rabbits are prey for a variety of _____.
    a. insects　　　　b. predators　　　c. plants　　　　d. trees

11. His _____ efforts will lead him to success.
    a. impolite　　　b. impulsive　　　c. constant　　　d. casual

[12~15] Choose the correct word for each definition.

unavoidable	organ	sweep	benefit	seed	suffer	relationship

12. to have pain or discomfort:

13. the connection between two things:

14. to move suddenly with a lot of force:

15. to receive an advantage:

• Have you ever heard of the native people of New Zealand?

The indigenous people of New Zealand, the Māori, have lived there since the 13th century. A Dutch explorer discovered the islands in 1642, and European settlers began arriving in the 18th century. By 1840, there were about 2,000 settlers and 125,000 Māori
5 living on the islands.

As more and more settlers arrived, Māori leaders began to worry. They asked Britain for protection from aggressive countries, such as France, as well as from British settlers who tried to steal their land. The British government agreed to sign an official treaty with the Māori chiefs—it was written in English and then translated into the
10 Māori language. The treaty was signed by the British and 43 chiefs in 1840 and was then transported across the country over the next eight months, where it was signed by more than 500 Māori chiefs.

The Treaty of Waitangi consisted of three main articles. The first gave the British monarchy sovereignty over all of New Zealand. The second allowed the chiefs to keep
15 their land, stating that they could sell it only to the British government. Finally, the treaty gave all Māori the same rights as British citizens. Unfortunately, translation problems soon caused controversy. The main problem was with the word "sovereignty," which means "having **complete** power over a group." However, it was translated into a Māori word meaning "the right to govern an independent group." Because of this, the British
20 believed the treaty gave them _____(A)_____. The Māori, however, believed it simply allowed the British to use their land.

These disagreements led to the New Zealand Land Wars, which were fought from 1845 to 1872. Hundreds were killed on both sides, but the British were eventually victorious. This led to the *confiscation of Māori land, a practice which continued into
25 the 20th century, until nearly all the land in New Zealand belonged to the British.

To help Māori tribes that had been mistreated, the Waitangi Tribunal was established in 1975. When the tribunal finds that the terms of the treaty were broken, the tribe receives compensation. Although debates regarding the Treaty of Waitangi continue today, it is considered one of the most important documents in New Zealand's history.

*confiscation: the official act of taking private things away from sb

WORD CHECK

Choose the correct words for the blanks from the highlighted words in the passage.

1. _____ to control people through laws
2. _____ acting in an angry and powerful way
3. _____ a formal agreement between countries
4. _____ a heated disagreement involving many people
5. _____ living or occurring naturally in a particular place

1 What is the passage mainly about?
   a. the origins of a country's official name
   b. a peace treaty between Britain and the Māori that saved many lives
   c. the background of and problems with a historical agreement
   d. a war that ended in New Zealand's independence

DETAILS

2 Which is NOT mentioned about the Treaty of Waitangi?
   a. which language it was written in
   b. the rough number of chiefs who signed it
   c. its contents
   d. how it is celebrated today

3 What is the best expression for blank (A)?
   a. protection from Māori leaders
   b. complete authority over the Māori and their land
   c. power to help the Māori in wars
   d. the temporary right to live on the islands

4 Put the following information about the Treaty of Waitangi in order, based on the passage.

   | c → _____ → _____ → _____ |

   a. An official treaty was agreed upon by the British and the Māori.
   b. Māori leaders asked Britain to protect them from other countries.
   c. European settlers began arriving on the islands the Māori lived on.
   d. Problems with the translation of the treaty's articles resulted in war.

5 Why was the Waitangi Tribunal set up?

   _____

SUMMARY

6 Complete the main idea of each paragraph using words from the passage.
   ▪ Paragraph 1: European _____ and the Māori lived together in New Zealand in the 19th century.
   ▪ Paragraph 2: The Māori wanted protection, so they signed a _____ with the British.
   ▪ Paragraph 3: _____ problems caused a disagreement about how much power Britain had.
   ▪ Paragraph 4&5: The disagreement led to 27 years of wars, and a tribunal was _____ in 1975 to help Māori tribes.

The American Civil War

By 1860, the Northern states and Southern states of the U.S. had developed into two different regions with opposing economic and political views. Politically, the South believed that the rights of the states were more important than a national government, while the North needed a central government to integrate the states into a union. The North and
5 South were most sharply divided over the issue of slavery, in particular, and the reason was that they had different economic interests; the North strongly opposed slavery, while the South was firm in its position on the necessity of slavery. These disagreements became the main reason for the American Civil War, which lasted from 1861 to 1865.

In the South, landowners, who only accounted for 5% of the population, operated
10 plantations to cultivate cotton, tobacco, and sugar cane, and more than 4 million slaves were essential for their sustainability. ■ Cotton agriculture burgeoned in the South during the industrial revolution with the development of the *cotton gin and other machines. ■ The Southern states accumulated their wealth by growing agricultural goods. ■ To do so, they relied on the low-cost labor of slaves and therefore resisted efforts to end the practice of
15 slavery. ■ With the growth in the production of industrial products such as textiles, paper, and metal, there was no longer a reliance on agriculture. Therefore, Northerners saw little need for slavery and were more likely to oppose it.

Against this backdrop, Abraham Lincoln, who was against slavery, became president in 1861. Seven Southern states broke away and attacked Fort Sumter at the end of the
20 same year, signaling the beginning of the American Civil War. By July 1864, the war was going favorably for the North with its victory at Gettysburg. The war finally ended when the Southern army surrendered in 1865.

The drawn-out war forced social and economic structures of the South to change. Plantations disappeared and capitalists from the North flocked to invest in the South, driving
25 the rapid growth of industries such as textiles, tobacco, and iron, as well as resources such as oil and coal. Between 1869 and 1870, American capitalism bloomed, with industrial production as a whole doubling.

*cotton gin: a machine that separates the seeds and other small objects from the fibers of cotton

1 According to the passage, which of the following was NOT a reason for the war between the North and the South?

ⓐ different political positions

ⓑ different economic foundations

ⓒ contrasting religious beliefs

ⓓ opposing opinions about slavery

2 Look at the four squares [■] that indicate where the following sentence could be added to the passage.

Meanwhile, the North had developed into an industrial capitalist society.

Where would the sentence best fit?

3 According to the passage, the Northern states opposed slavery because

(a) they had accumulated enough wealth

(b) they needed a central government

(c) they didn't need to rely on agriculture

(d) they thought it was bad for the economy

4 The word favorably in the passage is closest in meaning to

(a) agreeably   (b) advantageously   (c) fortunately   (d) appropriately

5 All of the following are mentioned in the passage as outcomes of the Civil War EXCEPT

(a) a change in the social structure of the South

(b) a movement of capital from the North to the South

(c) the nationwide growth in the labor force

(d) an overall increase in industrial production

6 ▆Directions▆ Look at the sentence in bold. It is the first sentence of a short summary of the passage. Choose THREE answers to complete the summary. Wrong answer choices use minor ideas from the passage or use information that is not in the passage.

The American Civil War was a war fought between the Northern and Southern states of the U.S. between 1861 and 1865.

(a) The most significant reason for the war was the election of Lincoln as president.

(b) The North and the South differed in their opinions about politics and the economy.

(c) Some slaves in the South escaped plantations before making their way to the North.

(d) Landowners only accounted for a small percentage of the South's population.

(e) The disagreements between the North and the South caused the war which ended in victory for the North.

(f) The war brought about considerable growth in industrial production in the U.S.

WARM-UP QUESTION • What are some children's stories you are familiar with?

Author Beatrix Potter is best remembered for writing the children's book *The Tale of Peter Rabbit* in 1902, although she was also a **skilled** and important amateur biologist, sheep farmer, and conservationist. The characters she created, like Benjamin Bunny and Squirrel Nutkin, touched children all over the world and sold millions of books, and the legacy of her other works can still be appreciated today.

ⓐ As a child, Beatrix was home schooled by governesses while her brother was sent away to be educated. ⓑ This made her develop a strong attachment to animals, and whenever she got the chance, she secretly brought them home as companions. ⓒ Studying their behavior, she practiced drawing them and created stories about them. ⓓ *The Tale of Peter Rabbit* was based on letters she wrote to the son of her former governess, and it was inspired by the actions of a real-life rabbit.

Sales of *The Tale of Peter Rabbit* had exceeded 50,000 copies within a year and Potter started to use the earnings to purchase real estate. Her purpose in acquiring land was to preserve the British countryside for the National Trust, an organization set up to protect and preserve land and buildings of beauty or historical importance. She not only bought land but also worked it as well. She learned how to farm, making a business out of raising sheep. In her work as a farmer, Beatrix aimed to make sure that traditional lifestyles and farming methods would not be forgotten.

When she died in 1943, Beatrix Potter left 4,000 acres of land to the National Trust to ensure that its beauty could remain unspoiled. Her legacy is now part of the Lake District National Park, thus helping to preserve for future generations not only the images of natural beauty in the works she penned but also the actual places that inspired her books.

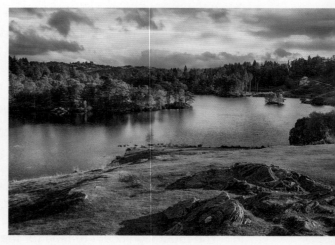

Choose the correct words for the blanks from the highlighted words in the passage.

1. _____ sth that is left behind for others after sb dies
2. _____ a connection to sth, often emotional
3. _____ property or land
4. _____ sb/sth that provides company; a friend
5. _____ engaged in as a hobby or a pastime

MAIN IDEA

1 **What is the passage mainly about?**

a. how Beatrix Potter educated herself

b. why Beatrix Potter supported the National Trust

c. how Beatrix Potter developed her love for nature

d. what made Beatrix Potter write children's literature

DETAILS

 2 **Where would the following sentence best fit in paragraph 2?**

> She was often alone and spent a lot of time in nature.

3 **Which is NOT true about Beatrix's literature according to the passage?**

a. The characters in her books include Squirrel Nutkin.

b. She was sent away to learn how to write children's literature.

c. *The Tale of Peter Rabbit* was originally written in the form of letters.

d. *The Tale of Peter Rabbit* was inspired by the activities of a real rabbit.

4 **What did Beatrix strive to preserve as a farmer according to paragraph 3?**

_____

5 **Which is NOT suggested about the Lake District National Park?**

a. It contains land Potter left to the National Trust.

b. It was being destroyed by industrialization.

c. Potter wanted to hand it down to future generations as it was.

d. Some of her literary works were inspired by its beauty.

SUMMARY

 6 **Match each topic to the correct paragraph in the passage.**

(1) Paragraph 1 •   • ⓐ the invaluable legacy of Beatrix Potter

(2) Paragraph 2 •   • ⓑ an overview of the works of Beatrix Potter

(3) Paragraph 3 •   • ⓒ the influence of Potter's early life on her writing

(4) Paragraph 4 •   • ⓓ Potter's contributions as a farmer and conservationist

If you were to listen to his mother, you would think that Terry Fox was "a very ordinary young man." Yet the legacy of his short life has been anything but ordinary. He has been the subject of two movies and two songs, has had a mountain
5　named after him, and has appeared on the face of a coin.

At the age of 18, Terry, a long distance runner and basketball player, was diagnosed with bone cancer. After he had his leg amputated above the knee, the suffering of other cancer patients he had seen convinced him that he should do
10　something. So, he decided to attempt to raise funds for cancer research by, incredibly, running across Canada and showing that he was no less of a person just because cancer had claimed one of his legs. On 12 April 1980, Terry Fox **set** out on his journey. Beginning at St. John's, his goals were to run to Vancouver, a distance of more than 8,000 km, and to raise $24 million in donations, one dollar for each Canadian.

15　Setting off on his journey with one natural and one artificial leg, Fox somehow managed to cover a distance of 42 km a day, approximately the length of a marathon. After 143 days he was well over halfway to achieving his goal of crossing Canada, but that was to be his last day of running. Terry's cancer had spread to his lungs, and he, along with his dream of finishing his "Marathon of Hope," was dying.

20　Before passing away, he helped set up the Terry Fox Run to commemorate his Marathon of Hope. Each year, people help raise funds for cancer research by collecting donations and running a short marathon in his memory. Upon Terry's insistence, the run is not competitive. There are no winners, no ribbons, and no prizes. Today, his run is held annually in over 60 countries and has raised more than $750 million for cancer research.
25　His hope for a cure for cancer lives on in those people his remarkable achievements continue to inspire.

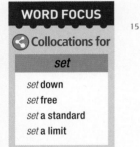

WORD FOCUS

◁ Collocations for

set

set down
set free
set a standard
set a limit

WORD CHECK

Choose the correct words for the blanks from the highlighted words in the passage.

1. _____ absolutely not; far from
2. _____ to remember sb/sth with an official event or ceremony
3. _____ man-made rather than natural
4. _____ to cut away and remove a limb
5. _____ involving the selection of a winner or loser

MAIN IDEA

1 **What is the best title for the passage?**

a. An Unbreakable Spirit Lives On

b. An Improbable Dream Comes True

c. No More Suffering from Cancer

d. An Absurd Journey across Canada

DETAILS

2 **When did Terry decide to attempt to raise money for cancer research?**

a. while he was traveling to Vancouver

b. when he was diagnosed with bone cancer

c. when he found out his cancer was spreading

d. after he saw the suffering of other cancer patients

3 **Why couldn't Terry finish his Marathon of Hope according to paragraph 3?**

_____

4 **Which is NOT true about the Terry Fox Run according to the passage?**

a. It is held to celebrate Terry's legacy.

b. It is a non-competitive event.

c. It was organized right after his death.

d. It is held every year in more than 60 countries.

5 **Which word best describes Terry's personality?**

a. hostile   b. resolute   c. sensitive   d. creative

SUMMARY

6 Use the words in the box to fill in the blanks.

| competition   legacy   diagnosed   half   funds   achieved |

Though his life was tragically short, Terry Fox's _____ has lived on for many years. _____ with cancer at age 18, which caused him to lose a leg, Terry decided to raise awareness and _____ for cancer research by running across Canada. He completed over _____ of his journey, but his condition had worsened. Remarkably, before dying, Terry helped set up an annual fundraising run, which takes place in over 60 countries worldwide.

WORD REVIEW TEST

[1~3] Choose the word that is closest in meaning to the underlined word.

1. The Malays are the indigenous people of Singapore.
   a. ordinary   b. important   c. native   d. professional

2. The two companies integrated their operating systems.
   a. adopted   b. combined   c. distinguished   d. administered

3. He was ordered to accumulate and analyze related data.
   a. extend   b. gather   c. donate   d. contribute

[4~7] Connect the matching words in columns A and B.

A	B
4. cause •	• a. a treaty
5. sign •	• b. controversy
6. translate •	• c. a country
7. govern •	• d. English into Korean

[8~11] Choose the best word to complete each sentence.

8. These ships are used to _____ our products.
   a. transport   b. mistreat   c. oppose   d. signal

9. Spam _____ 60% of all email communication.
   a. relies on   b. looks for   c. consists of   d. accounts for

10. Bad weather _____ the school to hold its graduation ceremony inside.
    a. forced   b. received   c. disappeared   d. cultivated

11. People _____ outside to watch the fight.
    a. discovered   b. flocked   c. earned   d. dedicated

[12~15] Choose the correct word for each definition.

invest	debate	burgeon	compensation	sustainability	mistreat

12. something given in return for damage caused:

13. to grow bigger and more powerful:

14. to spend money now to receive a profit later:

15. the ability to last for a long time:

[1~3] Choose the word that is closest in meaning to the underlined word.

1. Doctors were scheduled to amputate his left leg.
   a. deal with   b. look into   c. cut off   d. search for

2. When the king died, he left a legacy of peace and prosperity.
   a. property   b. money   c. reputation   d. inheritance

3. I purchased a small, convenient tablet PC.
   a. created   b. borrowed   c. bought   d. designed

[4~7] Connect the matching words in columns A and B.

A	B
4. raise •	• a. on a journey
5. hold •	• b. a dance competition
6. achieve •	• c. funds
7. set out •	• d. one's goal

[8~11] Choose the best word to complete each sentence. (Change the form if needed.)

exceed	unspoiled	commemorate	diagnose	skilled	journey

8. He was _____ with cancer, but recovered after treatment.

9. My dad is not an amateur but a(n) _____ carpenter.

10. It is a festival held to _____ Elvis Presley.

11. Carry-on baggage may not _____ two pieces.

[12~15] Choose the correct word for each definition.

conservationist	character	governess	acquire	donation	ordinary

12. not unusual or special:

13. an individual represented in a work of fiction (play, film, or story):

14. to obtain something as one's own:

15. a female teacher who lives with a rich family:

Many of our planet's most beautiful natural environments have been affected by the presence of humans. But Antarctica, which is about twice the size of Australia, remains a mystical land that is relatively untouched. This southernmost continent is valuable for several reasons. It is a place of unspoiled natural wilderness, great beauty, and important scientific research.

The wilderness of Antarctica is unlike that of a forest or jungle. You won't find any plants there, and there are very few animals. Also, it is a land of extremes: it is the coldest and driest of the continents, and it has the highest average elevation. About 98% of the continent is covered with a vast ice sheet that is larger than all of Europe. And because there are only a few thousand scientists living on the continent, it has been left almost entirely in its natural state.

In addition, the continent is treasured for its stunning beauty. Its pure white land expands endlessly toward the horizon, and at night, streamers of colored light, called an aurora, dance across the sky. There are also "polar nights," in which the night lasts for more than 24 hours. Before and after these long nights, the sun rises just barely above the horizon. It then moves as if it were rolling slowly along the ground, creating a beautiful and mysterious spectacle.

Antarctica is also extremely valuable as a scientific research site. In 1958, the Antarctic Treaty established the continent as a peaceful and cooperative international research zone. Each year between 1,000 and 4,000 scientists from over 27 countries live and work on research stations there. The experiments they perform help us to better understand our planet by providing important information on everything from the earth's ancient geological history to climate change.

Because of these intrinsic, unique qualities, all nations must cooperate to ensure that Antarctica is protected and preserved. It is **essential** that all activities that take place on the continent have a minimal environmental impact. That way, it can remain a valuable treasure for years to come.

WORD FOCUS

⟷ Antonyms for

essential

unimportant
optional
unnecessary
irrelevant

WORD CHECK

Choose the correct words for the blanks from the highlighted words in the passage.

1. _____ willing to work with others
2. _____ to make certain that sth occurs
3. _____ sth that is likely to impress
4. _____ to grow larger in number or size
5. _____ natural, untouched land

1 What is the best title for the passage?

   a. Antarctica: The Land of Extremes

   b. Antarctica's Untouched Natural Wilderness

   c. The Antarctic Treaty for the Protection of the South Pole

   d. Antarctica: Our Treasured Continent with Valuable Qualities

2 Which is closest in meaning to elevation?

   a. promotion   b. altitude   c. upturn   d. elaboration

3 Which is NOT mentioned as a beautiful aspect of Antarctica?

   a. the land covered with white ice

   b. the aurora in the sky

   c. the view before and after the polar nights

   d. the countless stars in the night sky

4 According to paragraph 4, how can experiments on Antarctica help us better understand the earth?

_____

5 Which is NOT true about Antarctica according to the passage?

   a. It is almost double the size of Australia.

   b. A few kinds of plants can survive in Antarctica.

   c. More than a thousand people are currently living in Antarctica.

   d. It was set up as an international research zone by the Antarctic Treaty.

6 Use the words in the box to fill in the blanks.

research wilderness aurora treaty extreme horizon nation

Values of Antarctica

Place of Nature	▪ No plants and few animals can live in its _____ environment. ▪ It remains almost completely in its natural state.
Place of Beauty	▪ You can see streamers of colored light, called a(n) _____, in the sky. ▪ Before and after polar nights, the sun moves beautifully along the _____.
Place of Science	▪ It was established as a peaceful and cooperative international _____ zone. ▪ Experiments that are done there provide important information about our planet and the environment.

In a place sometimes referred to as the "gateway to hell," pools of lava glow in the night and mirages dance above a blinding white layer of dried salt during the day. This is the Danakil Depression, one of the hottest places on earth. It covers around 100,000 square kilometers of land in northeastern Ethiopia.

5　　The Danakil Depression is part of a rift valley, a place where the earth's tectonic plates are moving apart and new crust is forming, which means the area is highly active geologically. It has volcanoes, hot springs, and colorful pools full of sulfur and other minerals. The heat from within the earth contributes to the extreme temperatures, which reach 55 degrees Celsius in summer. Once, the entire area was part of the Red Sea, but

10　buildups of lava separated it into an inland sea; later, the water evaporated in the dry climate, leaving vast deposits of salt.

In spite of its _____(A)_____ climate, the Danakil Depression has been useful in studying the evolution of life. Lucy, one of the oldest known early human ancestor fossils, was discovered here in 1974, confirming that humans **originate**d in Africa. Moreover,

15　the hot springs in the area are home to ancient species of microbes that live in extreme conditions that may be similar to those from earth's past or on other planets.

Modern humans have found a way to survive in the Danakil Depression. The Afar people move around the region, staying in portable wooden huts and herding animals. The Awash River gives them water and a little fertile land on which their animals can

20　graze. Their livelihood is based on salt trading—they cut out blocks of salt, load up their camels and donkeys, and walk for a week to sell them in town. Because their bodies are adapted to the heat, they can survive this journey with only a little bread and water.

Eventually, the Red Sea will likely cover the Danakil Depression again, but not for a few million

25　years. For now, it remains accessible to scientists—who are fascinated by the life forms that could give clues about life on other planets—and to the people who make their homes and livings there.

WORD FOCUS

≡ Synonyms for

originate

begin
emerge
arise

WORD CHECK

Choose the correct words for the blanks from the highlighted words in the passage.

1. _____ to change from a liquid to a gas
2. _____ easy to reach or use
3. _____ hot melted rock that emerges from a volcano
4. _____ able to produce healthy crops
5. _____ very great in degree

1 What is the best title for the passage?
   a. Life in One of Earth's Most Extreme Climates
   b. Understanding the Geology of Rift Valleys
   c. How the First Living Creatures Evolved in Deserts
   d. Studying the Struggle to Survive in the Danakil Depression

2 What is the best word for blank (A)?
   a. favorable   b. damp   c. inhospitable   d. frigid

3 What did the discovery of the early human ancestor fossil known as Lucy do?

_____

4 Which is NOT mentioned about the Danakil Depression?
   a. its approximate size
   b. how it was formed
   c. why its hot springs interest scientists
   d. the amount of salt collected there annually

5 Write T if the statement is true or F if it's false.
   (1) The tectonic plates of the Danakil Depression are highly stable.   _____
   (2) A river in the region provides water to the Afar people.   _____
   (3) The Danakil Depression will probably be covered by the Red Sea in a few   _____
       hundred years.

6 Match each topic to the correct paragraph in the passage.
   (1) Paragraph 1 •   • ⓐ the geology of the Danakil Depression
   (2) Paragraph 2 •   • ⓑ the lifestyle of the local people in the area
   (3) Paragraph 3 •   • ⓒ the location and appearance of the Danakil Depression
   (4) Paragraph 4 •   • ⓓ the region's relevance to the evolution of life
   (5) Paragraph 5 •   • ⓔ the present and future of the Danakil Depression

In 2015, the world's population included over 1.6 billion people who were 50 or older. This age group already makes up a larger percentage of the population than it did in the past, and experts predict that it will double in number by 2050. This shift is transforming economies everywhere.

Some see this change as a negative development. As the ratio of young people to old people goes down, taxes intended to support the elderly could become more burdensome to young workers. More people are taking money out of social security systems, while fewer are paying into them. In Europe, many nations now tax wages at 20 percent or more to make up for this. To meet the medical needs of an older population, more government resources must go towards health care, which could mean fewer resources are available elsewhere. In addition, as the number of elderly people grows, there will be a shortage of skilled workers trained to care for them. These difficulties make many people uneasy about the world's economic future.

Others, however, have a brighter view of the economic impact of the aging population. In general, this age group makes large contributions to the financial growth of countries. The economic activities of senior citizens are called the longevity economy, and they could compensate for the rise in public spending on health care. For example, Oxford Economics found that people over 50 make up 35 percent of the US population but produce 43 percent of the country's GDP and contribute 55 percent of the money spent on consumer goods. Seniors volunteer and donate to charities at higher rates than younger people, and many of them run small businesses, creating job opportunities for others. Because the longevity economy drives economic growth that benefits everyone, an aging population could actually pay for itself.

Longer life spans have created _____(A)_____, placing a **burden** on younger taxpayers, but they also mean that people can work productively for longer, which boosts the economy. Disagreements over the outcome persist, and the world waits to see whether the positives or negatives will win out.

WORD FOCUS

◀ Collocations for

burden

bear a *burden*
ease a *burden*
a **debt** *burden*
a **tax** *burden*

—
WORD
CHECK

Choose the correct words for the blanks from the highlighted words in the passage.

1. _____ a state in which there is not enough of sth
2. _____ a change in position or state
3. _____ the amount of time that a person or an animal lives
4. _____ to increase or enhance sth
5. _____ a relationship between two numbers or amounts

Making inferences from the context

To effectively understand a passage, we sometimes need to infer facts that are not directly mentioned. Some writers leave key points out of their passage and expect readers to infer them. So, it is important to consider exactly what the author is trying to say.

MAIN IDEA

1 What is the passage mainly about?

a. the effects of an aging population on the economy

b. reasons why people are living longer lives

c. health care programs for people over 50

d. the ways people today should prepare for retirement

DETAILS

2 Which is closest in meaning to make up for?

a. stand up for   b. substitute for   c. compensate for   d. account for

3 What is the longevity economy according to paragraph 3?

_____

4 Which of the following is NOT mentioned in the passage?

a. The number of people over 50 is expected to rise to 3.2 billion by 2050.

b. There will not be enough workers who can take care of the elderly in the future.

c. Senior citizens volunteer and donate to charities more than young people.

d. Many nations will give senior citizens more chances to get a job.

5 What is the best expression for blank (A)?

a. greater interest in hobbies

b. more awareness of spending habits

c. a stronger focus on "jobs for life"

d. the need for more medical care

SUMMARY

6 Use the words in the box to fill in the blanks.

| percentage | shortage | taxes | charities | opportunities | spend | aging |

The Longevity Economy

- Changing population
  - People over 50 make up a larger _____ of the population than in the past.
  - This influences economies worldwide.
- Negatives
  - Young people pay more _____ to support health care.
  - There is a(n) _____ of health-care workers.
- Positives
  - Seniors make and _____ more money than other age groups.
  - Some seniors run small businesses, which creates job _____.

WORD FOCUS

↔ Antonyms for

superior

inferior
low-grade
substandard

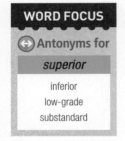

WARM-UP QUESTION • What do you think the term "freeconomics" means?

Everyone loves getting something for free, and these days it is easier than ever to receive a variety of free items. Companies give away free food, free T-shirts, even free cell phones. This might not seem like a smart thing for businesses to do, but it's actually a well-planned strategy based on something called "freeconomics."

5　　One basic practice of freeconomics is letting people try something once in order to make them become regular customers. For example, if you are given a free coffee at a café one morning, you might come back day after day to buy the same drink. This is the same reason a company might send you a small container of shampoo in the mail—they hope you will buy a full bottle the next time you go shopping. Another strategy of
10　freeconomics is to give consumers something for free, knowing they will then need to purchase something to accompany it. A phone company, for example, may give you a free cell phone, but you then need to pay for an annual plan.

　　The concept of freeconomics has been around for a while, but the Internet has made it more popular than ever. _____(A)_____ the cost of running an online business is so
15　low, websites are constantly offering free benefits in the hope of attracting more visitors. _____(B)_____ some people will simply take advantage of the free offerings, the business may be able to convince them to upgrade to more attractive paid services. This is known as the "freemium" strategy, a combination of the words "free" and "premium."

　　Some experts believe freeconomics will eventually change the way business takes
20　place. Already, any company with a **superior** product can benefit by giving potential consumers a free taste. And online, there are plenty of businesses, such as YouTube and Google, that don't need to sell anything to consumers at all. They simply attract millions of people to their websites with free services, and then they make their
25　profits from charging other companies to advertise on their site. These businesses make money, and we get to enjoy something for free.

WORD CHECK

Choose the correct words for the blanks from the highlighted words in the passage.

1. _____ again and again, without stopping
2. _____ to notify the public of a product or service
3. _____ to go along with sth or sb else
4. _____ to influence sb to do or believe sth
5. _____ a plan to achieve a specific goal

1 What is the passage mainly about?

   a. how to start an online business by yourself

   b. the strategy of making money by giving things away

   c. the models of the most successful online businesses

   d. ways of getting things for free on the Internet

2 What are the TWO strategies of freeconomics mentioned in paragraph 2?

_____

3 What is the best pair for blanks (A) and (B)?

	(A)	(B)		(A)	(B)
a.	Since	Before	b.	Though	If
c.	Because	Although	d.	Whether	When

4 Why does the writer mention YouTube and Google in paragraph 4?

   a. to argue that the "freemium" strategy is very effective

   b. to compare them with other businesses that aren't successful

   c. to criticize them for deceiving customers with false advertising

   d. to present examples of businesses that attract people with free services

5 Which is NOT a proper example of the freeconomics strategy according to the passage?

   a. Tom bought a dozen donuts at a store after he tasted a free one.

   b. Beth decided to subscribe to a magazine after she saw it on the bestseller list.

   c. Jason bought a musician's CD after he downloaded a free single on the Internet.

   d. Abby applied for a paid Internet service after she used it free for a month.

6 Use the words in the box to fill in the blanks.

upgrade	accompanying	free	regular	popularized	containers

Freeconomics

- Concept: the business strategy of giving away things for _____
- There are two main strategies:
  - give a free sample → the customer comes back to buy more
  - give a free item → make the customer pay for a(n) _____ product or service
- The Internet has _____ the use of freeconomics.
- The concept of "freemium":
  - give a free service → try to convince the customer to _____ to a paid service
- Freeconomics is having a strong effect on business practices.

WORD REVIEW TEST

[1~3] **Choose the word that is closest in meaning to the underlined word.**

1. My mom looks absolutely <u>stunning</u> in that blue dress.
   a. motivated   b. confident   c. annoyed   d. wonderful

2. The king once ruled over a <u>vast</u> empire.
   a. powerful   b. colonial   c. small   d. huge

3. He shared <u>valuable</u> information about the event.
   a. enlarged   b. beneficial   c. thoughtful   d. inspired

[4~7] **Connect the matching words in columns A and B.**

A		B
4. perform •		• a. in a field
5. make •		• b. a living
6. graze •		• c. with team members
7. cooperate •		• d. an experiment

[8~10] **Choose the best word to complete each sentence. (Change the form if needed.)**

accessible	fertile	continent	quality	evaporate	herd

8. The water _____ when it is boiling.

9. The shapes of the _____ of Asia and Africa have changed over millions of years.

10. The soil is _____ in this area, so it produces a lot of crops.

[11~12] **Circle the odd one out in each group.**

11. intrinsic   innate   inhale   inherent

12. portable   movable   mobile   flexible

[13~15] **Choose the correct word for each definition.**

separate	geological	inhospitable	untouched	adapt	clue

13. harsh and difficult to stay or live in:

14. not changed, damaged, or affected by humans:

15. to divide things so that they are not touching:

[1~3] Choose the word that is closest in meaning to the underlined word.

1. Older people <u>make up</u> a large proportion of Australia's population.
   a. express   b. increase   c. reduce   d. constitute

2. The speaker <u>convinced</u> them to vote for him for president.
   a. forced   b. persuaded   c. stopped   d. allowed

3. I have to <u>care for</u> my younger sister while my parents are away.
   a. pay for   b. stand for   c. look after   d. take advantage of

[4~6] Connect the matching words in columns A and B.

A		B
4. place •	•	a. a business
5. run •	•	b. to the latest version
6. upgrade •	•	c. a burden

[7~10] Choose the best word to complete each sentence.

7. He _____ thousands of dollars to an animal shelter every year.
   a. throws   b. donates   c. earns   d. wastes

8. Ever since I started college, Bob has been _____ telling me to study hard.
   a. already   b. lately   c. completely   d. constantly

9. The symptoms _____, so I went to the doctor again.
   a. persisted   b. stabilized   c. damaged   d. supported

10. The new trade agreement will _____ exports.
    a. work   b. boost   c. believe   d. undergo

[11~14] Choose the correct word for each definition.

predict   burdensome   transform   contribute   superior   combination

11. higher in quality:

12. to change the form of something:

13. to say what you think is going to happen:

14. more than one thing put together:

• Have you ever tried to communicate by whistling?

Whistling is often thought of as a simple action done without thinking, but some people use whistling to have **entire** conversations. Today, as many as 70 whistled languages are used around the world. Some are based on widespread spoken languages, like Spanish, while others are based on languages with few speakers. What they usually have in common is that they are used in mountainous areas or thick forests. In these surroundings, whistling can be heard more clearly and from farther away than shouting can.

Whistled languages are in danger of extinction because they tend to be used in isolated places. Take Sfyria, a whistled language from Antia, Greece, as an example. Its whistled sounds are based on the spoken sounds of Greek. Different combinations of whistled tones represent vowels, and consonants are reproduced by changing the tones of vowels. In the village where Sfyria originated, the population has declined to 37 people. Some residents have lost their teeth in their old age, so only six people able to whistle the language remain. In an attempt to save Sfyria, the people of Antia agreed to teach it to outsiders, something that was not done historically, and in 2012, they held a festival that attracted attention from around Greece and internationally.

Some groups have been fairly successful in preserving their whistled languages. On the island of La Gomera, near northern Africa, a whistled language called Silbo Gomero allows people to communicate in Spanish over long distances. It works by simplifying the sounds of Spanish into two whistled vowels and four whistled consonants. In the 1950s, the use of Silbo Gomero declined because of new communication technology, but in the 1980s, people began to realize what they were losing and took steps to protect it. They revived classes in schools and introduced programs for adults, and people of all ages on the island can use Silbo Gomero today.

So why fight to preserve a whistled language when we have long-distance communication tools? Each language carries information about the culture and history of the people who use it. As people everywhere begin to communicate in similar ways, will we remember the unique stories of people who saw, and talked about, the world in their own distinctive ways?

WORD FOCUS

⊜ Synonyms for

entire

whole
complete
total
full

WORD CHECK

Choose the correct words for the blanks from the highlighted words in the passage.

1. _____ a situation in which sth stops existing
2. _____ to make things less complicated
3. _____ easy to recognize because it is different from others
4. _____ to express or show sth
5. _____ existing or happening in many areas or among many people

1   What is the best title for the passage?

   a. How to Make a Wide Variety of Whistling Sounds

   b. Invented Languages Based in Western Europe

   c. Why Are Languages Becoming Extinct?

   d. Whistling: A Loud and Clear Way of Communication

2   Why are whistled languages used in mountainous areas or thick forests?

   _____

3   Which is true about Sfyria?

   a. The Greek language was created based on it.

   b. The vowels are expressed in combinations of tones.

   c. The number of people who can use it has been reduced to 37.

   d. The people of Antia do not want to teach it to outsiders.

4   What did people do to protect Silbo Gomero, according to the passage?

   a. They hosted a festival to introduce the language to outsiders.

   b. They started programs in Greek.

   c. They used new technology to keep its features.

   d. They offered classes for the language again in schools.

5   According to the passage, preserving whistled languages is important because _____

   _____.

   a. they are the only way to communicate from a distance

   b. they are necessary for old people in isolated places

   c. they are tools used to create strong bonds between people

   d. they contain the special stories of people who use them

6   Match each topic to the correct paragraph in the passage.

   (1) Paragraph 1 •   • ⓐ an endangered whistled language

   (2) Paragraph 2 •   • ⓑ an example of a well-preserved whistled language

   (3) Paragraph 3 •   • ⓒ the types and features of whistled languages

   (4) Paragraph 4 •   • ⓓ the value of whistled languages

WARM-UP QUESTION • If you could invent a language, what would you call it?

What would the world be like if everyone could communicate in one language? There was a man who tried to put this idea into practice—Poland's Dr. Ludovic Lazarus Zamenhof. His language, which was developed in the late 1870s and early 1880s, is known as Esperanto. It is a constructed language intended for use among people who speak different native languages. The word "Esperanto" means "a person who is hoping."

Zamenhof's goal was to create an easy and flexible language to foster peace and international understanding and to resolve many of the problems that lead to strife and conflict. It was to serve as an international auxiliary language—that is, as a universal second tongue—not to replace ethnic languages. The number of speakers grew rapidly over the next few decades, at first primarily in the Russian Empire and Eastern Europe, and then in Western Europe and East Asia.

There are three particular features that make Esperanto easy to learn compared to other languages. First, its system uses one letter for one sound, which means the spoken and written language can be learned and applied very quickly. Furthermore, just 16 grammatical rules need to be learned to understand nearly all the grammar of Esperanto. Finally, it is easy to form words from the most basic roots, and it is considered acceptable to create your own words.

It is estimated that around two million people are currently able to speak Esperanto. However, despite its easy-to-learn system, it was never made an official language of any country. This could be because Esperanto is frequently criticized for having vocabulary and grammar that are too closely related to Western European languages. Another common criticism of the language is that it has no culture. However, Esperanto is intentionally culturally neutral. It was intended to be a _____(A)_____ between cultures, not the _____(B)_____ of any one culture. Perhaps the future of the language depends on the outcome of the dispute between two sides within the Esperanto-speaking community: those who retain the original goal that Esperanto must become the universal second language and those who instead treat Esperanto as a kind of alternative lifestyle with no grand ambitions.

WORD CHECK

Choose the correct words for the blanks from the highlighted words in the passage.

1. _____ a strong desire to achieve sth
2. _____ to encourage sth to grow or develop
3. _____ giving extra help or support; secondary
4. _____ to judge or say bad things about sth/sb
5. _____ of a group having the same culture or language

1 What is the best title for the passage?

    a. The Complex Grammar of Esperanto

    b. Esperanto: Its Ambitions and Limits

    c. Esperanto: The Secrets of Its Success

    d. The Extraordinary Origins of Esperanto

2 Zamenhof's ultimate goal in inventing Esperanto was _____.

    a. to rid the world of illiteracy

    b. to help promote world peace

    c. to promote international trade

    d. to reduce the influence of American English

3 Which is NOT mentioned as a merit of Esperanto?

    a. its easy-to-learn system

    b. its simple grammar

    c. its accuracy

    d. its flexibility

4 What are the TWO things that are commonly mentioned as negative features of Esperanto?

_____

5 What is the best pair for blanks (A) and (B)?

	(A)	(B)
a.	facilitator	carrier
b.	barrier	advocate
c.	confusion	neutralizer
d.	disputer	identifier

6 Match each topic to the correct paragraph in the passage.

    (1) Paragraph 1 •   • ⓐ the goal of Esperanto and its scope

    (2) Paragraph 2 •   • ⓑ the easy-to-learn and flexible system of Esperanto

    (3) Paragraph 3 •   • ⓒ opinions about the value and prospects of Esperanto

    (4) Paragraph 4 •   • ⓓ Zamenhof's invention of Esperanto, an international language

WARM-UP QUESTION • Do you know any works of art by Rembrandt?

Rembrandt, a baroque artist, ranks as one of the greatest painters in Western history. Rembrandt Harmenszoon van Rijn was born on July 15, 1606, in Leiden, Netherlands. Combining a deep understanding of human nature with brilliant technique, he produced nearly 600 paintings. Rembrandt's work is famous for his command of light and dark, often using contrast to draw the viewer into the painting. This feature is best shown in *Night Watch*, his largest painting. It was completed in 1642, at the peak of the Dutch Golden Age.

Viewing the painting in person, one is struck by the extreme contrast between light and dark, which adds to the feeling of movement and depth. There is a man in the foreground of the painting carrying a spear that almost appears to be three-dimensional. This illusory depth shows what a genius Rembrandt was. His ability to use light and color, along with linear perspective, brings his paintings to life. However, if you were to look at a reproduction of *Night Watch* in a book, you would not be able to appreciate this. The spear, which seems so real in person, looks completely unremarkable in a photograph.

From the late 1630s, Rembrandt began to paint landscapes. These works focused on the darker side of nature, showing mysterious scenes such as huge fallen trees in a storm or threatening skies. Such characteristics can be found in his painting *Stormy Landscape*(1638). Toward the end of his life, Rembrandt painted some of his finest self-portraits, highlighting the effect that grief and sorrow had had on his face. They reflected his painful family life as opposed to his successful public career. The numerous self-portraits he produced give us a remarkable record of the aging process of his own facial features in addition to the changes of his own character.

Compared to other artists of his time, Rembrandt studied the world surrounding him more clearly and with greater insight. The consistently high standard throughout his work has earned Rembrandt the reputation of being a central figure in the golden age of Dutch art.

WORD CHECK

Choose the correct words for the blanks from the highlighted words in the passage.

1. _____ to give sb/sth a particular position or rating
2. _____ ability to see the truth about people or situations
3. _____ skillful control over an ability; mastery
4. _____ a copy of an original work
5. _____ unusual or causing people to take notice

READING SKILL

Guessing unknown words in context

We often find unknown words while reading a passage. In such situations, context gives us an idea of the possible meaning. We can also use our knowledge of how a word is constructed to work out its meaning.

MAIN IDEA

1 What is the best title for the passage?

a. The Colorful Life of Rembrandt

b. Renowned Artists of the Baroque Period

c. The Artistic Talents and Insights of Rembrandt

d. The Diverse Subjects of Baroque Paintings

DETAILS

2 According to paragraph 1, what is Rembrandt's work famous for?

_____

3 Which is closest in meaning to illusory?

a. vivid   b. false   c. illustrative   d. visible

4 Which is NOT mentioned as a feature of Rembrandt's work according to the passage?

a. appearance of depth

b. simple and calm subjects

c. landscapes with mysterious scenes

d. sadness in self-portraits

5 Which is true about Rembrandt according to the passage?

a. He produced more than 600 landscapes during the late 1630s.

b. The illusion of depth can be seen in reproductions of his works.

c. His family's support was the key to his success.

d. He was one of the main contributors to the golden age of Dutch art.

SUMMARY

6 Use the words in the box to fill in the blanks.

| pain   depth   subjects   consistent   nature   appreciate   reputation |

Rembrandt combined a profound understanding of human _____ with excellent technique to become one of the greatest artists in Western history. His work is famous for its use of differing tones of darkness and brightness to emphasize realistic movement and _____. Rembrandt's landscape work contained darker scenes, while his self-portraits showed his aging and personal _____. His insight and _____ brilliance has established him as a true master of art.

Baroque Art

After the Renaissance period had come to a close, European art was transformed with the dawn of the Baroque period around 1600. Baroque style originated in Rome and spread to most of Europe. The popularity and success of the Baroque movement was encouraged by the Catholic Church's populist movement.

5 In response to the challenge of the Protestant Reformation in the 17th century, the Catholic Church promoted traditional values of spirituality. The Church intended to use art as a tool of communicating its teachings to the illiterate as well as the educated. Many Baroque artists drew religious themes with direct, emotional involvement.

■ While the classical art of the Renaissance promoted human reason, Baroque art 10 focused on feelings and human sensitivity. ■ They did this by using strong contrasts in *value. ■ Employing different colors, they highlighted the power of brightness and darkness to show paintings in a more emotional way. ■ They also dealt with real life and common people as subjects rather than idealized, perfectly formed models like those used in the Renaissance period. Caravaggio and Annibale Carracci are two great figures of the Baroque 15 tradition, bringing a new richness to Italian painting. The peak point of Baroque art was the work of Gian Lorenzo Bernini, who dominated the High Baroque period with his energetic and spectacular art forms.

Although the Baroque movement actually started in Rome, it eventually influenced the artists of the Netherlands, France, Germany, and Spain, undergoing some change in each 20 of the countries to which it migrated. Dutch Baroque was based more on everyday life and led to the dominance of portraiture, landscape, and still life, as illustrated by the works of Vermeer and Rembrandt. In France, the Baroque style was used in the major art forms and promoted by the monarchy.

By the beginning of the 18th century, the Baroque style had been largely replaced 25 by the lighter Rococo movement that developed in the art world of Paris. Nevertheless, Baroque art and its influence continued to spread around the world.

*value: [art] degree of brightness and darkness

1 What is the passage mainly about?

ⓐ the characteristics of Baroque art

ⓑ the great artists of the Baroque period

ⓒ a comparison between Baroque and Renaissance art

ⓓ the power of the Catholic Church during the Baroque period

2 Why does the author mention the Protestant Reformation in paragraph 2?

  ⓐ to show the characteristics of Renaissance art

  ⓑ to suggest that the Baroque movement motivated it

  ⓒ to criticize the religious spirituality shown in Baroque art

  ⓓ to explain how the Catholic Church became involved in the Baroque movement

3 Look at the four squares [■] that indicate where the following sentence could be added to the passage.

In an attempt to appeal to the senses, Baroque artists tried to show emotion, variety, and movement in their artwork.

Where would the sentence best fit?

4 Which is NOT true about the features of Baroque art?

  ⓐ It deals with religious themes.

  ⓑ It emphasizes human feelings and sensitivity.

  ⓒ It describes common people and their real lives.

  ⓓ It uses bright colors rather than dark ones.

5 The word undergoing in the passage is closest in meaning to

  ⓐ generating   ⓑ experiencing   ⓒ preventing   ⓓ discovering

6 **Directions**   Look at the sentence in bold. It is the first sentence of a short summary of the passage. Choose THREE answers to complete the summary. Wrong answer choices use minor ideas from the passage or use information that is not in the passage.

Baroque art appeared as the result of the transformation of European art in the 17th century.

  ⓐ It was promoted by the Catholic Church.

  ⓑ The Baroque movement spread with the support of Protestants.

  ⓒ Its style in the Netherlands was loved mainly by the monarchy.

  ⓓ Its style developed with slight differences depending on the country.

  ⓔ Baroque art uses color to express emotions and focuses on real-life subjects.

  ⓕ Despite the appearance of the Rococo movement, it dominated art in the 18th century.

WORD REVIEW TEST

[1~4] Choose the word that is closest in meaning to the underlined word.

1. The program was designed to <u>foster</u> interest in science.
    a. argue   b. reduce   c. develop   d. contrast

2. None of the tribes speak the same <u>tongue</u>.
    a. gesture   b. culture   c. greeting   d. language

3. Every employee has a right to work in safe <u>surroundings</u>.
    a. environment   b. revenue   c. security   d. career

4. Not many people get to visit this <u>isolated</u> island.
    a. offshore   b. remote   c. volcanic   d. small

[5~8] Connect the matching words in columns A and B.

A		B
5. attract •		• a. a dying language
6. put •		• b. a problem
7. resolve •		• c. attention
8. preserve •		• d. an idea into practice

[9~12] Choose the best word to complete each sentence. (Change the form if needed.)

intentionally   auxiliary   estimate   criticize   extinction   revive

9. Many species are in danger of _____ due to environmental pollution.

10. The newly built shopping complex is expected to _____ the local economy.

11. The website did not _____ collect user information.

12. The amount of damage is _____ to be 10 billion won.

[13~14] Choose the correct definition of the underlined word in each sentence.

> **apply** *v.* **1.** to make a formal request for something: *I applied for a visa.* **2.** to be relevant or applicable: *The same laws apply to you.* **3.** to use in a particular situation: *apply the technology to practical business* **4.** to put on a surface: *apply a bandage to the wound*

13. He wants a job in which he can <u>apply</u> what he learned.   _____

14. These policies <u>apply</u> only to some of the workers.   _____

[1~4] Choose the word that is closest in meaning to the underlined word.

1. The <u>central</u> issue of the meeting was about human rights violations.
    a. recent   b. main   c. interesting   d. controversial

2. The doctor <u>employed</u> various herbal remedies to help cure his patients.
    a. searched   b. created   c. used   d. suggested

3. The government <u>transformed</u> the mountain village into a popular tourist attraction.
    a. destroyed   b. supported   c. changed   d. encouraged

4. Her report <u>highlights</u> the problem of noise pollution in big cities.
    a. studies   b. proves   c. explains   d. emphasizes

[5~7] Connect the matching words in columns A and B.

A		B
5. paint •   • a. to a close
6. come •   • b. landscapes
7. earn •   • c. a reputation

[8~10] Choose the best word to complete each sentence.

8. The company has _____ the world automobile market since 2015.
    a. painted   b. recollected   c. reflected   d. dominated

9. The writer is said to have deep _____ into the future of journalism.
    a. features   b. figures   c. insight   d. contrasts

10. We made a social networking site to _____ world peace.
    a. compare   b. promote   c. invent   d. replace

[11~14] Choose the correct word for each definition.

grief   spirituality   illiterate   foreground   brilliant   monarchy

11. a feeling of deep sorrow:

12. extremely clever or talented:

13. not knowing how to read or write:

14. a system in which a king or a queen rules:

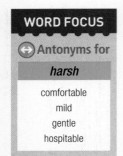

WARM-UP QUESTION • What are some examples of things people can learn from nature?

Human beings are endlessly innovative. Over the centuries, we have created many amazing ideas and inventions in order to solve some of the most difficult problems in history. However, the inspiration for many of these ideas and inventions came from nature. There is even a name for this field: biomimetics.

Biomimetics takes advantage of the fact that nature has been undergoing a process of trial and error for billions of years. Over that time, it has perfected many systems and processes that allow plants and animals to survive in challenging circumstances and **harsh** environments. Therefore, throughout history, humans have been looking to nature for solutions to problems and ideas for inventions. The bodies of birds, for example, inspired the design of airplanes, while the water-resistant qualities of lotus flowers have been copied to make waterproof paint.

Today, many new and exciting applications of biomimetics are being considered by scientists. For example, the strong silk used by spiders to make their webs may lead engineers to a flexible material that could be used to make bridge cables. Scientists have also been carefully studying animals that dive deep into the water to learn how they lower their brain temperatures and slow their metabolisms. It is hoped that this can help doctors find a way to treat seriously injured patients by putting their bodies into a similar state.

Biomimetic research is also being done on a wide variety of other ideas. A strong illustration is research on how plant leaves could be used as the model for a new kind of solar panel. A substance mussels use to attach themselves to rocks is similarly being studied and copied in order to create a non-toxic glue for surgeons. Ultimately, biomimetics creates a new kind of relationship between humans and nature. Instead of treating animals, plants, and microbes as resources to be controlled or harvested, we are now looking at them as teachers with valuable information to share.

WORD FOCUS

⟷ Antonyms for

harsh

comfortable

mild

gentle

hospitable

—
*WORD
CHECK*

Choose the correct words for the blanks from the highlighted words in the passage.

1. _____ a very tiny organism
2. _____ being original, imaginative, and unique
3. _____ sth that causes creativity or gives sb a good idea
4. _____ being hard to understand or deal with
5. _____ the practical use of sth

1 What is the best title for the passage?

　a. Biomimetics: Inspired by Nature

　b. People's New Approach to Preserving Nature

　c. Biomimetics: The Most Innovative Technology

　d. Applications of Creative Ideas to Control Nature

2 According to paragraph 2, how has nature perfected its systems and processes?

_____

3 The principle of biomimetics is that _____.

　a. humans exploit natural resources

　b. humans find innovative ways to help nature

　c. humans get ideas and solutions from nature

　d. humans survive in challenging circumstances and harsh environments

4 Which is closest in meaning to <u>attach</u>?

　a. detach　　　　b. link　　　　c. mix　　　　d. attempt

5 Which is NOT mentioned as an example of a biomimetic application?

　a. flexible bridge cables from spiders' strong silk

　b. a new diving suit copied from sea creatures

　c. a new kind of solar panel inspired by plant leaves

　d. a non-toxic glue for surgeons copied from mussels

6 Use the words in the box to fill in the blanks.

| resource | waterproof | solar | quality | lowered | inspiration | perfected |

Biomimetics

Definition	the science of using nature as the _____ for inventions
Reason	nature has _____ systems through trial and error
Examples	• the airplane's design based on bodies of birds • lotus flower properties copied to make _____ paint • spiderwebs being used to design material for bridge cables • non-toxic surgical glue similar to a substance used by mussels
Significance	leads humans to view nature as a teacher rather than a(n) _____

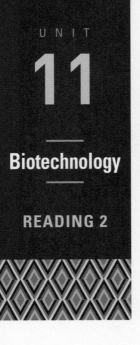

UNIT 11

Biotechnology

READING 2

WORD FOCUS

⟷ Antonyms for

dim

bright
brilliant
distinct
clear

WORD CHECK

WARM-UP QUESTION • Do you know any creatures that glow in the dark?

Nearly 200 years ago, Charles Darwin described the first time that he observed ocean water full of tiny bioluminescent organisms. He wrote that the sea was glowing with flickers of light. He also noted that the water still flashed with sparks of light after it was collected in a bottle. At the time, no one knew what caused the glow,

but bioluminescence has been the subject of much research since then.

Bioluminescence simply means light made by living things. Fireflies are a common example, but the phenomenon is found in some fish, mushrooms, bacteria, and other creatures as well. We now know that the light is made by chemicals called luciferins. The organisms light up when enzymes called luciferases interact with luciferin, and the varieties of luciferin in different creatures produce different colors of light.

Humans have occasionally made use of bioluminescence in the past. Glowing fungus growing on wood may have been used to mark trails through forests, and miners have used jars of fireflies to light their work underground. Unlike common light sources, bioluminescence produces almost no heat, so it is an attractive tool under many circumstances.

Today, even more applications of bioluminescence are possible. For example, it is used to warn of toxic substances in water. Bioluminescent bacteria in water grow **dim**mer when toxic substances are present, alerting people to test for contamination from pesticides or heavy metals. In addition, inventors are trying to create eco-friendly lamps from algae that glow when the water they live in moves. These lamps are expected to reduce energy usage and light pollution. In medical research, firefly luciferase is mixed with a dye that causes it to <u>emit</u> near-infrared light, which can be detected through relatively thick layers of tissue. This mixture is used to mark blood clotting proteins, making it easier to monitor the effectiveness of blood thinners.

Bioluminescence is older than the human species, but modern technology is giving it brand new uses. What was once a mysterious phenomenon is now helping us understand more about our bodies and the world around us, and hopefully allowing us to find ways to generate light with minimal environmental impact.

Choose the correct words for the blanks from the highlighted words in the passage.

1. _____ to make sb aware of sth important or dangerous
2. _____ a remarkable or unusual occurrence
3. _____ to make or produce sth
4. _____ a living thing
5. _____ to find or discover sth

1 What is the passage mainly about?

   a. the cause of bioluminescence and the ways humans use it

   b. where bioluminescent organisms are found and why they glow

   c. when bioluminescence evolved and why it is eco-friendly today

   d. the mystery of bioluminescence and how scientists struggle to understand it

2 Why does the writer mention Charles Darwin in paragraph 1?

   a. to explain how bioluminescent organisms make light

   b. to describe the amazing features of glowing creatures

   c. to show the effects of bioluminescence on the environment

   d. to emphasize his genius in bioluminescence research

3 According to paragraph 3, how is bioluminescence different from most other light sources?

_____

4 Which is NOT true about bioluminescence according to the passage?

   a. Bioluminescent organisms glow in various colors.

   b. People working in mines have made use of fireflies.

   c. When water is polluted, bioluminescent bacteria glow brighter.

   d. Special lamps containing glowing algae are being developed.

5 Which is closest in meaning to emit?

   a. split   b. release   c. absorb   d. depart

6 Use the words in the box to fill in the blanks.

produces	heat	dye	toxic	interacts	medical	eco-friendly

Bioluminescence

- the chemistry of bioluminescence: luciferin _____ with luciferase
  - → different varieties make different colors of light
- light with almost no _____ : attractive tool
  - → fireflies used for light in mines
- modern uses: technology opens new possibilities
  - → used to monitor water quality, create _____ lamps, and mark substances studied in _____ research

WORD FOCUS

⊜ Synonyms for

contain

hold
include
comprise
carry

WARM-UP QUESTION • How often do you change your smartphone?

You may have never heard of coltan, a kind of mineral found mostly in Africa. However, it **contains** tantalum, a rare metal that is probably a big part of your life. Tantalum is used to make tantalum *capacitors, which are an essential component of cameras, laptops, and cell phones. Not surprisingly, this makes tantalum highly valuable—so valuable, in fact, that a terrible conflict is being fought over it.

About 80% of the world's coltan is found in the Democratic Republic of the Congo. Currently, the country is in the middle of a violent armed conflict, and most of its coltan mines are controlled by military groups. They extract the coltan and sell it to neighboring countries, using the money to buy more weapons.

More and more people are buying electronic devices containing tantalum each year. To meet this demand, large amounts of coltan must be dug out of the earth. In many cases, small children are forced to work in the mines. Many farmers, whose fields have been destroyed in the fighting, are also employed by these mines. Although they receive a fair wage, they are often robbed of their pay by armed soldiers.

But humans aren't the only ones _____(A)_____. Wildlife in the area is also suffering. Endangered gorillas live in the area where coltan is mined, and they are often killed in the process of mining. The eastern region of the Congo was once home to thousands of eastern lowland gorillas; although the current population is unknown, it is believed to have been reduced by more than 50%.

The conflict in the Congo is a complicated situation without an easy solution. However, businesses can improve the situation by refusing to buy any coltan coming from military groups. Moreover, within the Congo, they can work to support legitimate coltan mines, making sure the profits are used to benefit communities.

Individuals can also help. By keeping our old electronic devices rather than buying new ones each year, we can reduce the demand for coltan. Then when we do upgrade to a newer model, we can recycle the old one or give it to charity instead of throwing it in the trash. Even the smallest efforts, when made by millions of consumers, can make a difference.

*capacitor: a small device used to store electricity in electronic products

Choose the correct words for the blanks from the highlighted words in the passage.

1. _____ to hire sb to perform a job
2. _____ to have serious pain or difficulty
3. _____ being legally and ethically honest and good
4. _____ one of a number of parts that make up sth
5. _____ to take or pull sth out of sth else, especially in a forceful way

1   What is the best title for the passage?

   a. Coltan Mining: Its Benefits for Humans

   b. Coltan: A Precious Metal for a Smart Generation

   c. Coltan: A Rare Metal for Africa's Hidden Jewelry

   d. Coltan Mining: Its Consequences and Solutions

DETAILS

2   Which is NOT true about coltan according to the passage?

   a. It is a mineral containing a rare metal called tantalum.

   b. It plays a role in the conflict in the Democratic Republic of the Congo.

   c. The government of the Democratic Republic of the Congo strictly controls its mines.

   d. Its demand is increasing as more and more people purchase digital devices.

3   What is the best expression for blank (A)?

   a. who benefit from coltan mining

   b. who are brought to the mines

   c. being killed for coltan mining

   d. being negatively affected

4   Which is NOT mentioned as a negative aspect of coltan mining?

   a. children being forced to work in the mines

   b. farmers getting robbed of their earnings

   c. gorillas being killed in the process

   d. mines being destroyed due to illegal mining

5   In what ways can businesses solve the coltan situation?

_____

SUMMARY

6   Use the words in the box to fill in the blanks.

| soldiers | improve | conflict | devices | weapons | recycle | wildlife |

Coltan is a mineral that contains a rare metal called tantalum. Tantalum is valuable because it is used in many electronic devices. Unfortunately, it is causing a violent _____ in the Democratic Republic of the Congo. Military groups extract it from mines and sell it to buy _____. Children and farmers are made to work in the mines, and gorillas that live nearby are being killed in the process of mining. However, there are some ways to _____ this situation. Businesses can stop buying coltan mined by military groups, and individuals can _____ or reuse old electronic devices.

WARM-UP QUESTION • Do you consider immigrants in Korea to be Korean?

Decades ago, foreigners were a rare sight in Korea, and many Koreans were actually proud of the fact that their country had very little **ethnic** diversity. But things have certainly changed. As Korea globalizes, the country's population is starting
5 to become more ethnically and racially diverse.

These changes came after the Korean War, when Korea began rebuilding and accepting foreign influences. The country grew rapidly over several decades and established itself as a global power in business and technology. Many foreigners started to move to Korea for
10 work, which gradually broadened the country's demographics. Meanwhile, many Korean families opened their arms to people from different backgrounds through transnational marriages.

Unfortunately, members of these multiracial families, along with many of the people who have immigrated to Korea, do not always find it easy to feel accepted. Some Koreans
15 still have a hard time thinking of people from other cultures as being Korean. There is a need to change these old attitudes and find a way for everyone to live in harmony.

One country that can serve as a model for Korea is Canada. Canada has the highest immigration rate in the world and was the first country to make multiculturalism an official national policy. Rather than expecting immigrants to adopt Canadian culture, the
20 Canadian government encourages (A) them to hold on to their own culture and identity. At the same time, (B) they expect the immigrants to embrace Canada as their new home and respect Canadian society.

A country does not automatically become multicultural by allowing a large number of immigrants through its borders. It requires truly understanding and accepting the
25 cultures and beliefs of newcomers. This process can take many years, as it is often quite difficult to change the attitudes of the older generation. Yet this is where Korea now finds itself, taking the first few steps on the road to multiculturalism.

WORD FOCUS

◀ Collocations for

ethnic

ethnic **difference**
ethnic **group**
ethnic **identity**
ethnic **minority**

WORD
CHECK

Choose the correct words for the blanks from the highlighted words in the passage.

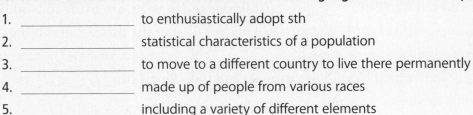

1. _____ to enthusiastically adopt sth
2. _____ statistical characteristics of a population
3. _____ to move to a different country to live there permanently
4. _____ made up of people from various races
5. _____ including a variety of different elements

READING SKILL

Separating fact and opinion
We tend to accept the information we read as truth, which is not desirable. When we read, we need to ask if the writer is using facts or opinions. Facts can be proven while opinions contain the writer's judgment.

MAIN IDEA

1 **What is the best title for the passage?**

   a. How Korea Can Be a Multicultural Country
   b. The Challenging Lives of Korean Immigrants
   c. The Drawbacks of a Multicultural Society
   d. Why Korea's Immigration Rates Are Rising

DETAILS

2 **Which is closest in meaning to hold on to?**

   a. control   b. keep   c. enhance   d. restrict

3 **What do (A) them and (B) they refer to in the passage?**

   (A) _____   (B) _____

4 **Write F if the statement is a fact, or O if it's an opinion.**

   (1) Immigrants came to work in Korea after the Korean War. _____
   (2) Old attitudes toward foreigners must be changed if we are to live in harmony. _____
   (3) Canada was the first country to make multiculturalism an official policy. _____
   (4) Understanding and acceptance of others is required to become truly multicultural. _____

5 **Which of the following is NOT true according to the passage?**

   a. Transnational marriages have contributed to racial diversity in Korea.
   b. Not all Koreans are accustomed to accepting immigrants in Korea as Korean citizens.
   c. The country with the highest immigration rate is Canada.
   d. Canada's policy on immigrants is to make them abandon their culture.

SUMMARY

6 **Use the words in the box to fill in the blanks.**

population   changed   model   attitudes   transnational   accepted

Globalization is helping Korea's _____ grow more diverse. This process began after the Korean War, when Korea began accepting foreign influences. The nation became a global leader and attracted many foreigners, who immigrated to Korea for various reasons such as job opportunities and _____ marriages. Unfortunately, multicultural families don't always feel _____ by Korean society. Koreans could benefit from using Canada as a(n) _____ of a balanced multicultural society. They should also try to understand the cultures of newcomers better.

WORD REVIEW TEST

[1~3] Choose the word that is closest in meaning to the underlined word.

1. The device's revolutionary <u>qualities</u> make it a must-have item.
   a. positions   b. features   c. indications   d. discoveries

2. The machine <u>generates</u> intense heat when it works.
   a. feels   b. loses   c. absorbs   d. creates

3. Atmospheric <u>contamination</u> is one of the growing concerns of the world's population.
   a. governor   b. pressure   c. pollution   d. condition

[4~7] Connect the matching words in columns A and B.

A		B
4. take	•	• a. with one another
5. make	•	• b. use of the opportunity
6. interact	•	• c. advantage of the tools
7. undergo	•	• d. hardships

[8~10] Choose the best word to complete each sentence.

8. A small amount of poison was _____ in her blood.
   a. invented   b. cured   c. detected   d. cloned

9. The crops were sprayed with a(n) _____ to kill harmful insects.
   a. pesticide   b. mist   c. harvest   d. infection

10. She _____ files containing the details of the event.
    a. glowed   b. attached   c. consumed   d. believed

[11~12] Circle the odd one out in each group.

11. injured   wounded   hurt   spoiled

12. valuable   replaceable   priceless   precious

[13~15] Choose the correct word for each definition.

underground   flexible   solution   metabolism   substance   minimal

13. bent easily without breaking:

14. the process of breaking down and using energy in the body:

15. of a minimum degree or amount:

[1~4] Choose the word that is closest in meaning to the underlined word.

1. Lisa was <u>employed</u> to design and create a website for the company.
   a. hired
   b. supported
   c. interviewed
   d. monitored

2. The <u>conflict</u> in the country must be stopped to protect innocent citizens.
   a. difference
   b. negotiation
   c. disobedience
   d. dispute

3. Nobody figured out the reason why she <u>refused</u> their favorable proposal.
   a. accepted
   b. eliminated
   c. declined
   d. confessed

4. The film festival has attracted a <u>diverse</u> audience from all over the world.
   a. varied
   b. young
   c. female
   d. few

[5~7] Connect the matching words in columns A and B.

	A		B
5.	support •	• a.	in harmony
6.	reduce •	• b.	its cost
7.	live •	• c.	the proposal

[8~11] Choose the best word to complete each sentence. (Change the form if needed.)

ethnic	electronic	destroy	immigrate	component	endangered

8. My family _____ to France last year to find a better life.

9. The ancient remains have been _____ by reckless construction.

10. _____ conflicts are regarded as the biggest problem in the country.

11. The government should establish regulations for hunting _____ species.

[12~15] Choose the correct word for each definition.

charity	globalize	border	armed	device	adopt

12. to choose to take up something:

13. an organization which raises money to help people who are ill, disabled, or poor:

14. a line dividing two countries:

15. carrying a weapon, usually a gun:

What are the basic requirements of life and what do we need next after those? When you answer these questions, you're doing the same kind of work that American psychologist Abraham Maslow did in his "hierarchy of needs" theory. The theory states that we must progress through various levels, satisfying the needs of each before being able to move on to the next. He thought individuals could eventually fulfill their potential if they could just satisfy several fundamental needs.

The most basic needs form the bottom of Maslow's hierarchy and are referred to as physiological needs. Physiological needs include our needs for food and shelter. Unless these are satisfied, we cannot move to the next level, safety needs. We need to feel secure in our environment, and this feeling of security usually means protection and freedom from fear. The third level is the need for love and belonging. People satisfy this need through their families and homes, as well as by joining and forming groups, making friends, and being part of a team.

In the fourth level, the need for esteem refers to people's need to be recognized. Here, they want to feel that others think highly of them; they may need praise and want to feel good about themselves. They may try to accomplish this by achieving set goals. Self-actualization, the fifth level, is the summit of Maslow's hierarchy of needs. It is the quest to reach one's full human potential. In this process people tend to have needs such as truth, justice, wisdom, and spiritual fulfillment.

Despite the appealing logic of Maslow's hierarchy, it seems to have some limits. Extensive research has suggested that there is little evidence for the ranking of levels and the argument of a definite hierarchy. Moreover, the concept of self-actualization is vague, and there's no evidence to show that every individual can reach it.

Maslow was the first psychologist to carry out **academic** research on human needs. He believed everybody should be encouraged to discover their vocations in life and endeavor to make life better. These are still important lessons today.

WORD CHECK

Choose the correct words for the blanks from the highlighted words in the passage.

1. _____ respect and admiration
2. _____ containing a lot of detail and depth
3. _____ sth that is needed
4. _____ a natural ability that could develop into sth special
5. _____ a system that ranks people or things by importance

1 **What is the passage mainly about?**

a. how to decrease desire in life

b. the classification of human needs

c. how to manage various needs in life

d. a successful way to achieve life goals

2 **Match the following needs with the corresponding level.**

(1) Level 2 •
(2) Level 3 •
(3) Level 4 •

• ⓐ need for fame, appreciation, and self-respect
• ⓑ need for finding safe circumstances and stability
• ⓒ desire to marry, have a family, and be part of a group

3 **Which is closest in meaning to quest?**

a. track   b. search   c. advance   d. capability

4 **According to paragraph 4, what is the criticism of self-actualization, the highest level of human needs?**

_____

5 **Write T if the statement is true or F if it's false.**

(1) According to Maslow, when lower needs are unmet, we can't reach our full potentials. _____

(2) There are arguments that a definite hierarchy is unlikely to exist. _____

(3) Maslow insisted that having a family is the highest value in one's life. _____

6 **Use the words in the box to fill in the blanks.**

| potential   definite   recognition   wisdom   basic   problems   theory |

American psychologist Abraham Maslow used his "hierarchy of needs" theory to show that we must meet a number of _____ needs before we can fulfill our _____. At the lower levels, we need food and shelter, the feeling of security, and a sense of belonging. After those, we need to receive _____ for our abilities before finally progressing to the state of self-actualization. Though it has some _____, Maslow's theory still teaches us important lessons.

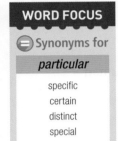
• How would you feel if you could see numbers in specific colors?

Richard Feynman, winner of the 1965 Nobel Prize in Physics, said that he saw letters in **particular** colors. For example, he saw the letter J in light tan, N in violet-blue, and X in dark brown. The
5 experience he described is known as synesthesia, a consistent association between two different types of sensory perception.

The word "synesthesia" is formed from Greek roots meaning "together" and "feeling." In general, the five senses are isolated from each other, but synesthesia results
10 when input from one sense or a specific type of perception stimulates another one as well. It can involve any combination of experiences of sight, hearing, touch, taste, and smell. One of the most common types is the association of colors with letters, numbers, or shapes, like the experiences described by Richard Feynman. Another is the association of colors with sounds. A famous example of this comes from the composer Franz Liszt,
15 who would tell his orchestra to play "a little bluer" or "not so rose!"

Studies have shown that people who have synesthesia are usually born with it or develop it in early childhood and that it can be inherited genetically. Researchers have also asked people to describe their synesthetic associations at points separated by long periods of time and found that _____(A)_____. For instance, a woman was
20 asked to list the colors that she associated with 100 different words. A year later, without warning, she was asked the same thing and gave the same answers for more than 90 of them.

Various theories exist about exactly what is happening in the brain when people experience synesthesia. Some researchers think that areas of the brain that deal with
25 the senses simply have more connections between them than usual. Others point out that information usually flows along neural connections in certain directions. Perhaps synesthesia results when this flow is regulated less than usual and some information moves "backwards."

Even with all our advances in studying the brain, we still have a lot to learn about
30 synesthesia. Through genetic studies and imaging techniques that show the brain in action, researchers hope to understand more. For now, its mystery is simply part of what makes it fascinating.

WORD FOCUS

⊖ Synonyms for
particular

specific
certain
distinct
special

WORD CHECK

Choose the correct words for the blanks from the highlighted words in the passage.

1. _____ to control an activity according to rules
2. _____ to make sth become more active
3. _____ highly or extremely interesting
4. _____ to receive certain traits from your parents
5. _____ to separate sb/sth from others

READING SKILL

Scanning

When scanning, we rapidly search for the information we are looking for. The idea behind scanning is to locate key words without reading the entire passage. When we locate a key word, we stop to read the entire sentence or section.

MAIN IDEA

1 What is the best title for the passage?

a. A Condition Created by Mixed Senses

b. Synesthesia: How the Brain Processes Colors

c. How Artists Improve Their Artistic Senses

d. Cultural Influences on Sensory Perception

DETAILS

2 Which is NOT a proper example of synesthesia according to the passage?

a. seeing the number three as blue

b. hearing someone's voice as orange

c. tasting salty foods as spicy

d. feeling music as circles

3 What is the best expression for blank (A)?

a. they are highly affected by cultural traits

b. they remain very similar

c. more men than women have synesthesia

d. they change significantly

4 According to paragraph 4, what might be happening to the flow of information along neural connections when people experience synesthesia?

_____

SUMMARY

5 Use the words in the box to fill in the blanks.

letters   results   connections   research   stimulates   information   genetics

Synesthesia

Definition	• a condition in which one type of sensory input consistently _____ another type
Examples	• Richard Feynman associated _____ with colors. • Franz Liszt associated sounds with colors. • People who have been studied describe the same associations at different points in time.
Theories	• Sensory areas of the brain have more _____ than usual. • The _____ flow along neural connections is less regulated than usual.

71

WARM-UP QUESTION • What can people do to save endangered animals?

5

Elephants are facing an increasing threat as human behavior continues to influence their natural environment. The number of people living in Asia and Africa has increased fourfold since 1900, which means that elephants have lost some of their habitat to human settlements. Although the sale of ivory was banned in 1990, the demand for it continues even today—this has led to a dramatic decline in elephant populations over the past few decades. The figures show a decrease in African elephant numbers of more than 90% since 1930, from more than 6 million to fewer than half a million today. There are even fewer Asian elephants left; only 35,000 to 40,000 still exist.

10

The threat of elephant extinction is worrisome in view of the vital role they play in the ecosystem. As huge and powerful consumers, elephants are a keystone species in their environment, affecting biodiversity in their regional habitats. They eat large quantities of woody vegetation and are thus responsible for clearing much of the land, contributing to the creation and maintenance of grasslands. These grasslands provide a habitat for other animals, such as antelopes.

15

_____(A)_____, elephant dung is important to the environment. Baboons and birds pick through elephant dung for undigested seeds and nuts, and dung beetles reproduce in these deposits. The nutrient-rich dung also helps damaged soil to recover. Finally, it is a vehicle for spreading seeds over a wide area. It's important to note that some seeds will not grow unless they have passed through an elephant's digestive system.

20

In an attempt to save elephants, environmental groups have declared them an endangered species and have been using drones and GPS technology to protect them from hunters. Moreover, many elephant habitats have been conserved as national parks. Most environmentalists believe, however, that the parks are too small and too isolated from each other to allow elephant populations to recover. What most people do agree on is that without serious international cooperation, elephants face the threat of extinction in the near future.

25

< ● ● 03 ● >

WORD CHECK

Choose the correct words for the blanks from the highlighted words in the passage.

1. _____ trees and other plants
2. _____ to announce through official channels
3. _____ to make a child or a copy of sth
4. _____ all the animals and plants in an area and how they are related
5. _____ the natural environment where an animal or plant lives and grows

1 What is the best title for the passage?

    a. How Species Disappear

    b. Saving the Habitats of Animals

    c. A Keystone Species Facing Extinction

    d. The Most Powerful Animals in Africa

DETAILS

2 According to paragraph 1, what has happened due to the continuing demand for ivory?

_____

3 What is the best word for blank (A)?

    a. However   b. Accordingly   c. Nevertheless   d. Furthermore

4 Which of the following is NOT true according to the passage?

    a. Elephants contribute to the creation and maintenance of grasslands.

    b. Elephants can be a serious threat to antelopes.

    c. Elephant dung is a source of food for some animals.

    d. An elephant's digestive system helps some seeds to grow.

5 What is the problem with national parks used to conserve elephant habitats?

_____

6 Which of the following is NOT mentioned in the passage?

    a. the current conditions facing elephants

    b. physical characteristics of elephants

    c. the ecological impact of elephants

    d. measures taken to protect elephants

SUMMARY

7 Match each main point to the correct paragraph in the passage.

    (1) Paragraph 1 •   • ⓐ Efforts are being made to protect elephants and their habitats.

    (2) Paragraph 2 •   • ⓑ Elephants are a keystone species, so their loss could have a huge impact on the environment.

    (3) Paragraph 3 •   • ⓒ Humans are causing African and Asian elephant populations to decline.

    (4) Paragraph 4 •   • ⓓ Elephant dung plays an important role in the ecosystem.

WARM-UP QUESTION • Have you ever heard of the Great Barrier Reef?

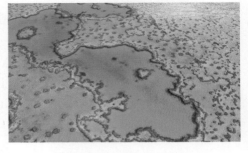

Over the centuries, people have built some impressive structures, but did you know that the largest known thing built by any group of living creatures is the Great Barrier Reef off the coast of

5 Australia? This giant reef system covers 344,400 square kilometers and can be divided into 2,900 individual reefs, all made by tiny coral polyps building hard shells around themselves. The reef was designated a World Heritage Site in 1981, and it both supports a diverse community of wildlife and serves as an important **indicator** of the health of our planet.

10 The Great Barrier Reef is home to vast numbers of species, including 400 types of coral and 1,500 species of fish, and gives shelter to endangered species such as dugongs and sea turtles. The reef system helps regulate the global climate because coral polyps absorb carbon dioxide as they build their shells. It also keeps large waves and rough weather away from the coast of Australia, making it a safer place for people to live.

15 Currently, the reef faces several dangers to its health and even survival. ⓐ It is a popular tourist destination, and careless visitors are harming it. ⓑ Human activity on the land is also threatening the reef, as fertilizers and pesticides wash into the water, making it toxic for some organisms. ⓒ Since coral stays healthiest within a specific range of temperatures, warmer water puts it at risk of disease and death, which in turn endangers

20 the entire ecosystem that depends on it. ⓓ

To protect the reef, people in Australia have established conservation programs and guidelines for tourists. Both government and private funds are being used to improve water quality around the reef and address specific threats to its health. Tourists visiting the reef can contribute to conservation efforts by choosing tour options certified by

25 Ecotourism Australia to avoid causing damage to the area.

For years, people have thought of the Great Barrier Reef primarily as a tourism site. It is also a wonderland for biologists and nature lovers. However, before we view it as anything else, we need to remember that it is a collection of delicate living things that can easily be injured and must be protected.

WORD FOCUS

☰ Synonyms for

indicator

sign
signal
gauge
index

WORD CHECK

Choose the correct words for the blanks from the highlighted words in the passage.

1. _____ the act of protecting the natural environment
2. _____ the place where you are going
3. _____ to give sb/sth a particular status
4. _____ extremely large
5. _____ not strong and easily damaged

1 **What is the passage mainly about?**

   a. the features and conditions of an impressive natural site
   b. safety considerations when traveling to wild places
   c. how technology is being used to protect sea creatures
   d. whether ecotourism helps or harms delicate ecosystems

DETAILS

2 **How can coral polyps help regulate the global climate?**

_____

3 **Where would the following sentence best fit in paragraph 3?**

   But most serious is the danger posed by climate change.

4 **If a place gives shelter, it means** _____.

   a. it gives medical treatment and care
   b. it provides a safe place to live
   c. humans created it
   d. it is difficult to clean

5 **Write T if the statement is true or F if it's false.**

   (1) The Great Barrier Reef has not yet been listed as a World Heritage Site.   _____
   (2) The Great Barrier Reef protects the coast of Australia from big waves.   _____
   (3) Coral is not affected by the water temperature it lives in.   _____
   (4) Government money is being used to conserve the Great Barrier Reef.   _____

SUMMARY

6 **Match each topic to the correct paragraph in the passage.**

   (1) Paragraph 1 •   • ⓐ protection efforts
   (2) Paragraph 2 •   • ⓑ benefits of the reef
   (3) Paragraph 3 •   • ⓒ the location and size of the reef
   (4) Paragraph 4 •   • ⓓ the importance of our attitude
   (5) Paragraph 5 •   • ⓔ threats to the reef

WORD REVIEW TEST

[1~4] Choose the word that is closest in meaning to the underlined word.

1. The view from the <u>summit</u> of the mountain is superb.
    a. hillside   b. peak   c. valley   d. ice cap

2. His speeches on education policies were too <u>vague</u>.
    a. straightforward   b. touching   c. boring   d. unclear

3. Despite his <u>consistent</u> failures, he didn't give up.
    a. apparent   b. economic   c. constant   d. initial

4. His reassurance left me feeling <u>secure</u> and comfortable.
    a. depressed   b. safe   c. nervous   d. afraid

[5~7] Connect the matching words in columns A and B.

A		B
5. think •		• a. highly of him
6. regulate •		• b. students' needs
7. satisfy •		• c. the flow of water

[8~11] Choose the best word to complete each sentence. (Change the form if needed.)

endeavor	progress	associate	appealing	inherit	composer

8. We always _____ to please our customers.

9. Mozart is a famous _____ of chamber music.

10. She always _____ the smell of roasting meat with camping.

11. He _____ his acting talent from his father.

[12~16] Choose the correct word for each definition.

physiological	fulfill	evidence	neural	combination	involve

12. to achieve a desired result:

13. something used to prove a belief:

14. to include something as a necessary part:

15. relating to nerves or the nervous system:

16. relating to how the body works:

UNIT 13

[1~4] Choose the word that is closest in meaning to the underlined word.

1. The organization's goal is the <u>conservation</u> of wildlife.
   a. atmosphere   b. habitat   c. preservation   d. shell

2. This document is to <u>certify</u> that the above-mentioned person has completed his internship.
   a. deny   b. achieve   c. protest   d. verify

3. Babies <u>depend on</u> their parents for survival.
   a. agree on   b. rely on   c. base on   d. act on

4. The economy is beginning to <u>recover</u>.
   a. get better   b. get worse   c. get away   d. get out

[5~8] Connect the matching words in columns A and B.

A		B
5. face •		• a. the quality of something
6. absorb •		• b. a vital role
7. improve •		• c. a challenge
8. play •		• d. carbon dioxide

[9~12] Choose the best word to complete each sentence. (Change the form if needed.)

maintenance   endangered   delicate   contribute   reproduce   regulate

9. Most fish _____ by laying eggs.

10. The hawksbill sea turtle is listed as a(n) _____ species.

11. Research shows that regular exercise _____ to a long, healthy life.

12. The restaurant has been shut down for _____.

[13~15] Choose the correct word for each definition.

settlement   deposit   ban   quantity   threaten   species

13. to make something illegal:

14. to be likely to cause harm:

15. a group of houses, or places, where humans live:

The 6th century B.C. witnessed the development of rapid changes in ancient Greece as rival city-states competed with each other for power. The two most powerful of these city-states, Athens and Sparta, developed different systems of government, each with unique characteristics that would have profound effects on the future of ancient Greece.

Athens entered its golden age with the introduction of democracy ruled by the "**common** people." A council, known as the Boule, had both executive and administrative control. Members of this council were chosen by lot, rather than by election, and served for one year. Any citizen over the age of 30 was eligible, but only men born in Athens were considered citizens. An assembly, open to all citizens, passed laws and made policy decisions.

Meanwhile, an *oligarchy had developed in Sparta, which was ruled by two kings from two great aristocratic houses and a group of five powerful leaders known as Ephors, who had full administrative and executive authority with the privilege to control the kings of Sparta. These Ephors were, in turn, chosen by the Spartiates, native male Spartans over the age of 30 who formed the top level of society and were the only inhabitants to receive full legal and political rights.

Despite their apparent positive attributes, the systems of these two city-states had their own limitations. In Sparta, slaves outnumbered their masters by seven to one, and the city could not function without the work of enslaved people. Accordingly, Spartan society suffered from a fear of a slave rebellion and developed a military state in order to retain stability. In contrast to Sparta, democracy was able to be established in Athens. But it was a limited democracy, where only a small percentage of men had influence, women could not vote, and slaves did most of the work.

*oligarchy: government by a small group of people

WORD FOCUS

◀ Collocations for

common

common approach
common sense
common error
fairly *common*

WORD CHECK

Choose the correct words for the blanks from the highlighted words in the passage.

1. _____ able to have or do sth because of having the right qualifications
2. _____ one who lives in a particular place
3. _____ having a strong influence or effect
4. _____ the condition of being steady and unchanging
5. _____ to be greater in number than sb/sth

Identifying comparison and contrast

Passages discussing two or more examples or ideas often compare and contrast them in order to better explain their qualities. Comparisons look at how they are alike, while contrasts look at how they are different.

MAIN IDEA

1 **What is the passage mainly about?**

a. the origin of democratic society

b. rivalry between two Greek city-states

c. two governmental systems of ancient Greece

d. characteristics of Athenian and Spartan citizens

DETAILS

2 **Which is NOT true concerning the two Greek city-states?**

		Athens	Sparta
a.	governmental system	democracy	oligarchy
b.	executive power	council	kings
c.	full political rights	native male citizens over 30	native male citizens over 30
d.	existence of slaves	yes	yes

3 **Which is closest in meaning to retain?**

a. limit   b. endanger   c. preserve   d. compromise

4 **Why did Sparta establish a military state according to paragraph 4?**

_____

5 **Why is Athenian democracy called a limited democracy according to paragraph 4?**

_____

SUMMARY

6 Use the words in the box to fill in the blanks.

| rival   privilege   native   limited   executive   military   government |

The 6th century B.C. saw the rise of two city-states in Greece—Athens and Sparta—with very different systems of _____. Athens introduced a form of democracy with an executive and administrative council, along with an assembly. In contrast, Sparta developed an oligarchy controlled by kings and five Ephors with administrative and _____ power. Both systems had their problems: Sparta needed the _____ to retain stability, while Athens had only a(n) _____ democracy.

Plato's *Republic*

Ancient Athens was home to the first democracy, and it produced some great thinkers. As democracy started to fail, the philosophers of the time tried to figure out why and to think of ways to fix it. One of these philosophers was Plato(427-347 B.C.), a student of Socrates(469-399 B.C.). Plato began to doubt the democracy of his time and tried to think
5 of a better option.

In one of his most famous works, *The Republic*, Plato proposed his ideal society. It was based on what he saw as the four virtues of the state: wisdom, courage, self-discipline, and justice. He designated a different class of people to fulfill three of these virtues. The wise would rule as "philosopher kings," the brave would act as "guardians," the
10 self-disciplined would do "manual work," and the whole of society would work together toward justice.

Plato saw people as being naturally inclined to serve one of these roles because of their soul. The soul, according to Plato, is divided into three parts: the rational, the will, and the appetite. If the individual is governed more by the rational element, he or she is suited
15 to rule. Someone who is governed by the will would make a good guardian, and a person governed by the appetite would make a good worker.

The ultimate goals of society, for Plato, were fulfillment of needs and happiness. ■ Everyone has needs, and everyone has abilities. ■ Therefore, he felt, society must work together to satisfy the needs of all people. ■ When everyone specializes in their occupation
20 and then exchanges the fruits of their labor with others, all people can meet their needs and be happy. ■ Crucially, Plato believed that the perfect society would occur only when kings became philosophers or philosophers were made kings, as it is the wisdom of their decision-making that is the key to the success of a social unit.

Plato's *Republic* was designed to put in place a system that addressed the innate
25 characteristics of the people. Although its aim seems too impractical to become reality, his thoughts laid the foundations of Western philosophy.

1   What is the passage mainly about?

ⓐ how to fulfill the happiness of all citizens

ⓑ the features of an ideal society as proposed by Plato

ⓒ Plato's contribution to the understanding of human nature

ⓓ the relationship between individual citizens and society

2 According to the passage, which is NOT true about Plato's beliefs about the soul?

   (a) People are inclined to perform a role according to the character of their soul.

   (b) It is divided into the rational, the will, and the appetite.

   (c) Someone who is led by the rational would be a good ruler.

   (d) Someone who is governed by the will would be good at labor.

3 Look at the four squares [■] that indicate where the following sentence could be added to the passage.

But people don't have the range of abilities required to meet all of their individual needs.

Where would the sentence best fit?

4 According to the passage, Plato

   (a) thought the democracy of the 4th century B.C. was perfect.

   (b) insisted that all people should have four virtues.

   (c) wrote that hierarchical society is more stable than democratic society.

   (d) believed wisdom is the decisive element in establishing an ideal society.

5 The word impractical in the passage is closest in meaning to

   (a) technical   (b) mental   (c) unrealistic   (d) intellectual

6   Directions Look at the sentence in bold. It is the first sentence of a short summary of the passage. Choose THREE answers to complete the summary. Wrong answer choices use minor ideas from the passage or use information that is not in the passage.

Plato's *Republic* proposed an ideal society ruled by a philosopher king.

   (a) As a student of Socrates, Plato began to think about democracy.

   (b) Plato's ideal society included a highly specialized division of roles based on people's natural abilities.

   (c) Plato believed that the perfect citizen had rationality, will, and appetite.

   (d) Plato recommended that people work together to fulfill needs and be happy.

   (e) Plato believed that an ideal society would be attained when kings and philosophers were as one.

   (f) Plato wanted a democratic system that worked despite the different characteristics of its citizens.

WORD REVIEW TEST

[1~3] Choose the word that is closest in meaning to the underlined word.

1. His most outstanding attribute was his kindness.
    a. limit   b. feature   c. right   d. appearance

2. What do you think the world would be like if he ruled the country?
    a. governed   b. forced   c. voted   d. invaded

3. You can figure out a word's meaning by using context clues.
    a. mention   b. satisfy   c. address   d. understand

[4~7] Connect the matching words in columns A and B.

A		B
4. pass •		• a. it into two
5. divide •		• b. one's needs
6. meet •		• c. a law
7. lay •		• d. the foundations

[8~11] Choose the best word to complete each sentence.

8. You are _____ to vote if you are 19 years old.
    a. courageous   b. eligible   c. limited   d. executive

9. He is _____ to get upset over small things.
    a. inclined   b. obvious   c. annoying   d. obliged

10. Susan was _____ as the new chief of staff.
    a. revised   b. elaborated   c. captured   d. designated

11. Blacks _____ the other races in South Africa.
    a. attest   b. delay   c. outnumber   d. cancel

[12~14] Choose the correct word for each definition.

innate   ideal   profound   stability   administrative   lot

12. a state of being perfect:

13. something chosen at random to make a decision:

14. connected with organizing the work of the government:

NE능률의 모든 교재가 한 곳에 - 엔이 북스

NE_Books

NE능률의 유초등 교재부터 중고생 참고서,
토익·토플 수험서와 일반 영어까지!
PC는 물론 태블릿 PC, 스마트폰으로 언제 어디서나
NE능률의 교재와 다양한 학습 자료를 만나보세요.

✓ 필요한 부가 학습 자료 바로 찾기
✓ 주요 인기 교재들을 한눈에 확인
✓ 나에게 딱 맞는 교재를 찾아주는 스마트 검색
✓ 함께 보면 좋은 교재와 다음 단계 교재 추천
✓ 회원 가입, 교재 후기 작성 등 사이트 활동 시 NE Point 적립

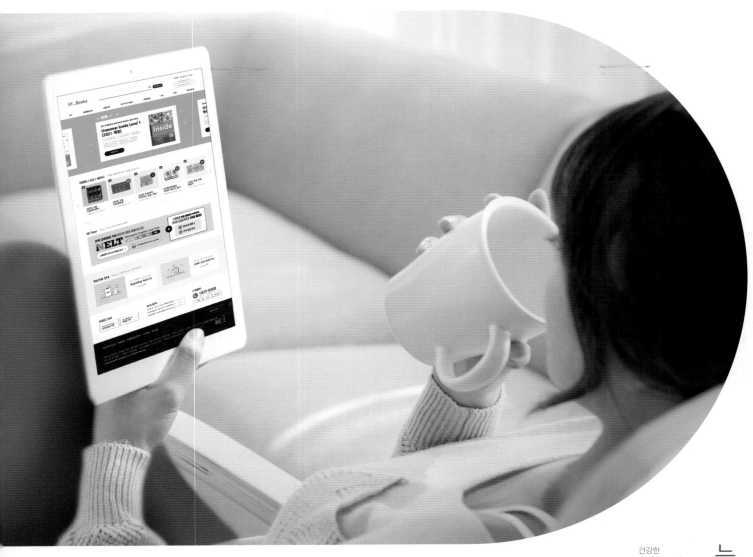

건강한
배움의 즐거움

NE 능률

영어교과서 리딩튜터 능률보카 빠른독해 바른독해 수능만만 월등한 개념 수학 유형 더블
NE_Build & Grow   NE_Times   NE_Kids(굿잡,상상수프)   NE_능률 주니어랩   아이챌린지

READING EXPERT

A 5-LEVEL READING COURSE for EFL Readers

5

NE _ Neungyule

Answers & Explanations

READING
EXPERT

A 5-LEVEL READING COURSE for EFL Readers

5

Answers & Explanations

Reading 용어 및 지시문

Ⅰ. 글의 구조와 관련된 용어

- **passage(지문):** 한 주제를 다룬 하나의 짧은 글을 말한다. 여러 개의 단락이 모여 한 지문을 구성한다.
- **paragraph(단락):** 글쓴이가 하나의 주제에 대하여 전개해 나가는 서로 연관된 여러 문장의 집합을 말한다. 흔히 들여쓰기로 단락과 단락 사이를 구분한다.
- **main idea(요지):** 글쓴이가 말하고자 하는 바, 즉 중심이 되는 견해로 보통 문장으로 표현된다.
- **topic sentence(주제문):** 글쓴이의 중심적 견해를 담고 있는 문장으로 각 단락에는 topic sentence가 있다.

Ⅱ. 지시문

- **What is the best title for the passage?** (이 글에 가장 알맞은 제목은?)
- **What is the passage mainly about?** (이 글은 주로 무엇에 관한 내용인가?)
- **What is the main idea of the passage?** (이 글의 중심생각[요지]은 무엇인가?)
- **What is the best word [expression] for blank (A)?** (빈칸 (A)에 들어갈 말로 가장 알맞은 것은?)
- **What is the best pair for blanks (A) and (B)?** (빈칸 (A)와 (B)에 들어갈 말을 짝지은 것 중 가장 적절한 것은?)
- **Which is closest in meaning to appreciated?** (appreciated의 의미와 가장 가까운 것은?)
- **What does the underlined part mean?** (밑줄 친 부분이 의미하는 것은?)
- **What can be inferred from the underlined part?** (밑줄 친 부분에서 유추할 수 있는 것은?)
- **Which of the following is NOT mentioned in the passage?** (다음 중 이 글에서 언급되지 않은 것은?)
- **Which of the following is NOT true according to the passage?** (다음 중 본문의 내용과 일치하지 않는 것은?)
- **Write T if the statement is true or F if it's false.** (진술이 참이면 T, 거짓이면 F를 쓰시오.)
- **Where would the following sentence best fit?** (다음 문장이 들어갈 위치로 가장 알맞은 곳은?)
- **Use the words in the box to fill in the blanks.** (상자 안의 단어를 골라 빈칸을 채우시오.)
- **Match each topic to the correct paragraph in the passage.** (각 주제와 본문의 단락을 알맞게 연결하시오.)

UNIT 01.
Culture

READING 1   p. 8~9

WORD FOCUS integrate

unite 통합[결합]하다 / blend 섞다 / incorporate 통합하다

WORD CHECK

1. temporary   2. elaborately   3. float
4. old-fashioned   5. rebellion

▶ declare: to officially announce sth, especially about a legal or political topic

정답

1. d   2. ⓒ   3. They symbolize equality and integrate all of Colombia's citizens, regardless of race or ethnicity.
4. a   5. c   6. rebellion, freedom, parade, white

해석

흑과 백의 축제는 다채로운 행사처럼 들리지 않을 수도 있지만, 사실은 다채롭다! 이 연례행사는 1월 4일부터 6일까지 콜롬비아의 파스토에서 열리고, 공들여 디자인된 장식 차량 및 의상으로 이루어진 행진을 포함한다. 이것은 남미에서 가장 오래된 축제 행사 중 하나이기도 하며, 2002년에 콜롬비아 문화유산의 일부로 공식 선언되었다.

축제의 초창기 기원은 17세기로 거슬러 올라간다. 1607년에 레메디오스라는 도시에서 노예 반란이 있었던 이후, 그 지역의 노예들은 하루의 특별 휴일을 요구하기 시작했다. 이에 대해, 그 당시 콜롬비아를 지배하던 스페인 왕은 1월 5일을 모든 노예들이 일시적인 자유를 즐길 수 있는 날로 선언하였다. 그 소식을 듣자마자, 그 지역의 노예들은 석탄으로 도시의 하얀 벽을 검게 만들며 음악과 춤으로 축하했다. 그들의 주인들은 즐거움에 동참하기 위해 심지어 자신의 얼굴을 까맣게 칠하기까지 했다. 다음 날에는 노예들이 자신의 얼굴을 하얗게 칠하는 것으로 응답했다. 이러한 방식으로, 한 위대한 전통이 시작되었다.

19세기 중반 언젠가, 이 전통이 파스토에 들어오게 됐고, 현대의 흑과 백의 축제가 탄생했다. 요즘에는 1월 4일에 큰 행렬로 축제가 시작된다. 사람들은 형형색색의 복고풍 옷으로 차려입고 도시의 거리를 걷는다. 축제의 두 가지 주요 행사는 1월 5일과 6일에 열린다. 첫 번째는 '흑의 날'이다. 모든 인종과 민족적 배경의 사람들이 검은색 페인트로 자신을 칠하고, 관현악단은 거리에서 무료 공연을 한다. 다음 날인 '백의 날'에는 사람들이 서로에게 하얀 가루를 던진다. 이 두 가지 행사는 평등을 상징하며 인종이나 민족성에 상관없이 모든 콜롬비아 시민들을 통합시킨다.

흑과 백의 축제는 남미에서 가장 활기가 넘치는 축제 중 하나로 여겨지며, 전 세계에서 온 방문객들을 환영하는 상냥한 사람들로 가득하다. 이 축제는 모든 사람이 즐거운 시간을 보내기 위해 다 같이 모일 수 있는 시간이다. 하지만 더 중요한 것은 이것이 콜롬비아의 인종적 다양성과 통합을 기념한다는 것이다.

구문 해설

[11행] In response, the king of Spain, **who** ruled Colombia at that time, declared January 5th a day [*on which* all slaves could enjoy temporary freedom].

▶ who는 the king of Spain을 선행사로 하는 계속적 용법의 관계대명사
▶ on which는 관계부사 when으로 바꿔 쓸 수 있음

[13행] **Upon hearing** the news, the region's slaves celebrated with music and dancing, *blackening* the city's white walls with coal.

▶ upon v-ing: ~하자마자
▶ blackening 이하는 부대상황을 나타내는 분사구문

[27행] It is a time [**when** everyone can come together to have fun].

▶ when은 a time를 선행사로 하는 관계부사

READING 2   p. 10~11

WORD FOCUS method

manner 방법, 방식 / technique 기법, 방법 / process (만드는) 과정 / style 방식

WORD CHECK

1. sacred   2. typical   3. texture   4. reflect
5. monument

▶ generation: the period of time between the birth of a person and the birth of that person's children

정답

1. b   2. d   3. c   4. (1) T (2) F (3) F   5. Because bread stands for all the basic needs of life.   6. (1) ⓓ (2) ⓐ (3) ⓒ (4) ⓔ (5) ⓑ

해석

고대 이집트인들은 인상적인 무덤과 기념물로 기억된다. 그러나 오늘날 모든 이집트 가정의 일부인, 고대 이집트인의 삶에서 덜 유명한 것이 있다. 그것은 밀로 만든 플랫브레드(납작한 빵)인 아이시 발라디(aish baladi)이다. 고대 이집트에서 밀은 주요 식량원 중의 하나였고 신의 신성한 식물로 여겨졌다. 밀을 재배하는 전통은 아이시 발라디를 만들어 냈는데, 그것은 이집트 문화의 독특한 부분으로 남아 있다.

아이시 발라디는 이집트 어디에서나 볼 수 있다. 카이로에서 여러분은 갓 구워진 아이시 발라디를 파는 사람에게서 절대로 멀리 떨어져 있지 않다. 플랫브레드는 둥글고 가운데는 공기로 불룩하다. 그것들은 위에 빻은 밀이 있으며 부드럽고 푹신한 것부터 마른 것까지 여러 질감으로 나온다. 통밀로 만들어지기 때문에, 그것들은 이 곡물이 지닌 높은 섬유질, 비타민, 그리고

3

미네랄 함량에 대한 영양상의 이점을 가지고 있다. 식사 때에, 아이시 발라디는 샌드위치를 만들거나 부드러운 음식과 소스를 퍼내는 데 안성맞춤이다.

고고학은 아이시 발라디가 아주 오랫동안 존재해 왔다는 것을 보여주었다. 고대 무덤의 예술 작품은 오늘날 만들어지는 둥근 플랫브레드와 똑같아 보이는 음식의 그림을 담고 있으며, 심지어 보존된 빵 조각들도 발견되었다. 고대 이집트인들은 반죽에 야생 효모를 넣고, 그 반죽을 나일강의 붉은 진흙으로 만든 화덕에 넣고 구워서 빵을 만들었다. 아이시 발라디의 조리법과 그것을 굽는 방법은 수천 년 동안 그대로 유지되어 오고 있다.

고대부터 빵의 중요성은 이집트의 언어와 문화에 영향을 주었다. 아이시 발라디라는 이름도 이 점을 반영한다. 그것은 '빵'을 나타내는 대표적인 아랍어와 매우 다르다. 그것은 '전통적인'(baladi)과 '삶'(aish)을 의미하는 단어들로부터 형성되었다. 2011년 이집트 혁명 도중 '빵, 자유, 사회적 정의'라는 구호가 사용되었는데, 빵이 삶의 모든 기본적인 욕구를 나타내기 때문이다.

많은 음식들처럼, 아이시 발라디는 단순한 식사 이상의 것이다. 그것은 세대에 걸친 전통과 수천 년의 역사를 나타낸다. 아이시 발라디가 여전히 현대의 삶에서 큰 역할을 하기 때문에 그것의 이야기는 계속해서 늘어나고 있다.

구문 해설

7행
The wheat-growing tradition brought about *aish baladi*, **which** has remained a unique part of Egyptian culture.
▶ which는 aish baladi를 선행사로 하는 계속적 용법의 관계대명사

16행
Artwork in ancient tombs includes pictures of food {that looks just like the round flatbread [made today]}, and ....

17행
The ancient Egyptians made bread **by**
  adding wild yeast to their dough
  and
  baking the dough in ovens [made from the Nile's red mud].
▶ by v-ing: ~함으로써

UNIT 02.
Health

READING 1   p. 12~13

WORD FOCUS   mind

an open mind 열린 마음 / keep in mind ~을 마음에 담아두다, ~을 명심하다 / come to mind (갑자기) 생각나다 / in one's mind ~의 마음속에

WORD CHECK
1. cognitive   2. hinder   3. troubling   4. excessive
5. diagnose
▶ enhance: to make sth work better

정답

1. c   2. It tends to get overworked.   3. d   4. c   5. b
6. overuse, imbalance, mental, Memorize, exercising

해석

치매는 기억력과 집중력에 영향을 끼치는 잘 알려진 장애이다. 치매 환자들은 전화번호나 사람들의 이름처럼 간단한 것들을 기억하는 데 자주 어려움을 느낀다. 치매가 일반적으로 노인들에게 진단이 되기는 하지만, 최근에 10대 및 20대와 30대 성인에게도 치매와 비슷한 증상이 늘고 있어 문제가 되고 있다. 이런 새로운 유형의 치매는 '디지털 치매'라고 불려오고 있다.

왜 '디지털'이라고 부르는가? 그것은 스마트폰의 과도한 사용과, TV와 컴퓨터 화면 앞에서 긴 시간을 보내는 것 때문으로 여겨지고 있다. 이러한 기기들이 지나치게 사용되면, 논리 및 추론을 담당하는 좌뇌가 과도하게 사용되는 경향이 있다. 그동안, 기억, 집중, 사고 처리와 같은 인지 기능을 돕는 우뇌는 거의 활용되지 않는다. 뇌가 사용되는 방법에 있어서 이러한 불균형은 기억력 문제를 야기한다. 이 때문에 몇몇 국가의 전문가들은 교실에서 스마트폰과 다른 전자 기기를 금지할 것을 권고하고 있다.

또한, 사람들은 요즘에 전화번호와 다른 단편적인 정보들을 머릿속 대신 스마트폰에 저장하는 경향이 있다. 그 결과로 발생한 정신적 자극의 결핍이 기억력과 두뇌 발달을 저해한다는 것이 제기되어 왔다. 이 견해는 10대의 90% 이상이 스마트폰을 소유하고 있는 한국에서 디지털 치매 발생이 걱정스러울 정도로 증가하고 있다는 사실에 의해 뒷받침된다.

그러면 디지털 치매에 맞서 싸우기 위해 여러분은 무엇을 할 수 있을까? 우선, 필요할 때만 디지털 기기를 사용하도록 노력하라. 또, 가족과 친구들의 전화번호를 외우는 것도 기억력을 예리하게 유지하는 좋은 방법이다. 책을 읽는 것과 일기를 쓰는 것도 두뇌를 지속적으로 자극하는 좋은 활동이다. 마지막으로, 유산소 운동은 두뇌의 혈액 순환을 강화하고 정신 건강에도 좋다. 이러한 활동들은 여러분이 건강한 생활을 하고 디지털 치매의 희생자가 되는 것을 막도록 도와줄 수 있다.

구문 해설

2행
Dementia patients often **find** *it* **hard** *to remember* simple things, ...
▶ find + 목적어 + 형용사: ~을 …하다고 느끼다[여기다]
▶ it은 가목적어, to remember 이하가 진목적어

13행
This imbalance in [**how** the brain is used] leads to memory problems.

4

▶ how가 이끄는 절은 전치사 in의 목적어로 쓰인 관계부사절
(선행사 the way와 관계부사 how는 둘 중 하나를 생략)

(26행) These activities can **help** you **lead** a healthy life and **avoid** becoming a victim of digital dementia.
▶ help + 목적어 + (to)-v: ~이 …하도록 돕다

READING 2　　　　　　　　　　p. 14~15

WORD CHECK

1. utilize　2. emphasis　3. practitioner　4. defect
5. innovation
▶ synthesized: being made from combinations of different things through a chemical process

정답

1. b　2. c　3. b　4. d　5. (1) science (2) herbs
(3) machine (4) diagnostic

해석

　　때로는 두 사람이 같은 문제를 보고 두 개의 매우 다른 해결 방법을 생각해 낼 수 있습니다. 서양 의료진과 중국, 즉 동양 의료진의 경우가 바로 그러하죠. 우리 기자가 무엇이 그들을 구분 짓는지 더 알아보기 위해 두 명의 의사와 좌담을 했습니다.

기자: 스미스 박사님, 서양의 의사들이 의학에 대해 갖는 일반적인 접근법에 대해 설명해 주세요.

스미스 박사: 현대 의학은 다른 자연 과학과 같은 시기에 발달했습니다. 우리는 의학을 과학으로 생각하기 때문에, 의학에 대한 우리의 이해는 신중하게 계획된 실험실 실험에 좌우됩니다. 마찬가지로, 우리가 개발하는 치료약은 대개 실험실에서 화학적으로 합성된 약품의 형태로 나옵니다.

기자: 우 박사님, 동양 의학은 방금 스미스 박사님이 설명하신 것과 어떤 차이가 있습니까?

우 박사: 서양 의학이 과학이라면, 동양 의학은 예술이라고 생각할 수 있습니다. 예술이 문화적 전통에 기반을 두고 여러 세기를 거쳐 발전하는 것과 마찬가지로, 우리의 의료술도 그러합니다. 또한, 동양의 치료약은 보통 합성된 약품보다는 순수한 자연의 약초를 주의해서 투여하는 것을 이용합니다.

기자: 스미스 박사님, 서양식 의학 접근법의 한 가지 단점이라면 뭐가 있을까요?

스미스 박사: 안타깝게도, 우리는 인체를 하나의 기계로 간주하고, 그래서 각각의 질병을 기계의 결함으로 보게 됩니다. 결함이 있는 부분을 수리하거나 교체하면, 기계는 정상적으로 기능하게 됩니다. 하지만, 인체는 서로 연결된 복잡한 조직망이기 때문에, 인체가 전체로서 어떻게 작용하는지 그 실체를 아직 완전히 이해할 수는 없습니다.

기자: 우 박사님, 동양식 접근법의 단점은 어떻습니까?

우 박사: 특정 질병의 원인에 대한 연구 및 조사에 충분한 주의를 기울이지 않는 것이라고 생각합니다. 서양 의사들은 효과적인 진단 도구를 재량껏 사용하는데, 이건 많은 동양 의사들에게 부족하거나 그들이 관심을 갖지 않는 점이죠.

기자: 여러분은 앞으로의 의학에 대해 어떻게 예측하십니까?

우 박사: 미래에는 두 전통이 좀 더 긴밀히 협력할 것으로 생각합니다. 둘 다 중요한 혁신을 일궈낼 것이고, 이 둘이 협력한다면 상당히 효과적일 수 있습니다.

스미스 박사: 네, 저도 그렇게 생각합니다.

구문 해설

(6행) Dr. Smith, explain for us the general approach [**that** Western physicians take ∧ toward medicine].
▶ that은 the general approach를 선행사로 하는 목적격 관계대명사

(21행) **Just as** art is based on cultural tradition and evolves through the centuries, **so** does our practice of medicine.
(V) (S)
▶ Just as ~ so …: ~한 것과 마찬가지로 …하다 (so 뒤에서 주어와 동사가 도치됨)

(29행) Unfortunately, we **view** the human body **as** a machine, and *it follows that* each illness ….
▶ view A as B: A를 B로 바라보다[간주하다]
▶ it follows that ~: 당연히 ~라는 결과가 나오다

(42행) Western doctors have powerful diagnostic tools at their disposal, something [**that** many Chinese doctors either lack ∧ or simply aren't interested in ∧].
▶ that은 something을 선행사로 하는 목적격 관계대명사

WORD REVIEW TEST

UNIT 01　　　　　　　　　　p. 16

1. b　2. d　3. b　4. b　5. d　6. a　7. c　8. a　9. a
10. c　11. c　12. unity　13. method　14. respond
15. coal

UNIT 02　　　　　　　　　　p. 17

1. d　2. b　3. d　4. c　5. b　6. a　7. d　8. c
9. defect　10. reasoning　11. diagnostic
12. concentration　13. evolve　14. dementia
15. circulation　16. sharp

UNIT 03.
Media

READING 1   p. 18~19

WORD FOCUS   encourage

discourage 낙담시키다 / dissuade 단념시키다 / hinder 방해하다

WORD CHECK

1. beg   2. supporter   3. shatter   4. keep in touch with   5. activism
▶ potential: a possibility that could develop into sth special

정답

1. d   2. b   3. He created it to help homeless people get involved with social media, tell their stories, and contact support services.   4. a   5. c   6. voice, posting, share, inspired

해석

여러분은 친구들과 연락하거나 일상 사진과 정보를 공유하기 위해 아마 페이스북이나 트위터 계정을 사용할지도 모른다. 하지만 소셜 미디어는 훨씬 많은 것을 할 수 있는 잠재력이 있다. 예를 들면, 어떤 사람들은 불우한 사람들에게 발언권을 주려고 소셜 미디어를 사용하기 시작했다. 이렇게 소셜 미디어는 단지 정보를 공유하는 재미있는 방법 그 이상이 될 수 있고, 사람들의 삶에 실제 변화를 가져올 수도 있다.

세계적으로 인정받는 사회 운동가 마크 호바스가 바로 그것을 해 오고 있다. 2008년에 웹 사이트를 개설한 이후 그는 미국과 캐나다 전역에 걸쳐 집 없이 살아가는 사람들의 이야기를 공유해 왔다. 그는 시애틀에서 노숙자들을 인터뷰하고, 그 대화를 유튜브에 게시하면서 시작했다. 그는 영상의 높은 조회수에 용기를 얻었고, 지지자들이 있다는 것을 깨닫자 자동차 여행을 하며 미국 전역에 있는 사람들을 인터뷰했다. 그리고 그는 2010년에 노숙자들이 소셜 미디어에 참여하고, 그들의 이야기를 전하고, 지원 서비스와 접촉할 수 있도록 돕기 위해 또 다른 웹 사이트를 개설했다.

호바스는 노숙자들에게 문제가 있을 때 아무도 그들에게 귀 기울이고 싶어 하지 않는다고 말했다. 그 역시 한때 노숙자였기 때문에 이 점을 알고 있다. 그 당시 그는 상상하는 것 이상으로 더 무기력함을 느꼈다고 말했다. 하지만 지금은 그의 활동 덕분에 사람들이 귀를 기울이고 있다. 많은 사람들이 심지어 행동으로 옮기기 시작했다. 캘거리에 있는 사람들은 거리에서 21년간 생활했던 도니라는 남자와 그의 인터뷰를 보고 그 남자가 집을 찾을 수 있게 도와주었다. 또, 호바스의 웹 사이트에서 영상을 보고 난 뒤 아칸소 주에 있는 한 농부는 저소득층 가정을 위한 식량을 생산하는 데 사용되도록 40에이커의 땅을 기부했다.

소셜 미디어가 일상생활에 대한 개인의 의견이나 생각을 단순히 공유하는 데 가장 흔히 사용되기는 하지만, 그 가능성은 무한하다. 대부분의 사람들은 노숙자들을 그저 돈을 구걸하는 거리의 사람으로 생각한다. 그들은 그 사람들의 분투나 삶을 재건하려는 그들의 노력에 대해서는 거의 듣지도, 생각하지도 않는다. 호바스의 일은 소셜 미디어가 고정 관념을 깨부수고 도움이 필요한 사람들에게 발언권을 줄 수 있는 방법을 보여주는 아주 좋은 예이다.

구문 해설

[8행] **Since** starting a website in 2008, he has been sharing the stories ....
▶ Since ... 2008은 접속사가 생략되지 않은 분사구문 (= Since he started ...)

[20행] When people in Calgary saw his interview with a man [named Donny], **who** had lived on the street for 21 years, they helped him find housing.
(S / V / O)
▶ who는 a man named Donny를 선행사로 하는 계속적 용법의 관계대명사

[25행] Most people just **think of** the homeless **as** street people [begging for money].
▶ think of A as B: A를 B로 생각하다[여기다]

READING 2   p. 20~21

WORD FOCUS   habit

break a habit 습관을 고치다 / change a habit 습관을 바꾸다 / become habit 습관이 되다 / an old habit 오래된 습관

WORD CHECK

1. accurate   2. statistic   3. household   4. install
5. audience
▶ criticism: comments showing disapproval of sth

정답

1. c   2. When you watch TV, you push a personalized button that activates the people meter and push it again when you are finished viewing.   3. ⓑ   4. c
5. number, diary, attached, sample

해석

텔레비전 프로그램의 성공이나 실패에 대해 논할 때, 사람들은 대개 시청자의 수를 언급한다. 이것은 기업들이 광고 결정을 하는 데 사용하므로 중요한 통계치이다. 그런데 여러분은 이 숫자가 어떻게 정해지는지 궁금하게 여긴 적이 있는가? 실제로 그렇게 하는 것을 다루는 온전한 분야가 있는데, 그것은 시청자층 조사라고 알려져 있다.

물론, 전 세계 모든 사람이 어떤 특정한 시간에 무엇을 시청하는지 알아내는 것은 불가능하다. 그 대신에, 표본 시청자가 조사된다. 미국에서, 이

러한 표본은 25,000세대로 구성된다. 과거에는 이 가족들에게 시청 습관에 대한 일지를 적어 일주일에 한 번 제출하도록 요구하였다. 그리고 1990년대에는, TV 미터 덕분에 이 방식이 폐기되었다. 이것은 가족이 무엇을 시청하는지를 정확히 기록하기 위해 각 세대의 텔레비전에 부착된 장치였다.

그러나 요즘 대부분의 TV 미터는 '피플 미터'로 대체되었다. 이 장치는 좀 더 자세한 정보 수집이 가능하다. 예를 들어, 그것들은 각 세대의 개별 구성원이 시청하는 것을 추적할 수 있다. TV를 보기 위해 앉을 때, 여러분은 피플 미터를 작동시키는 개인 전용 버튼을 누르는 것이다. 여러분은 시청이 끝나면 다시 버튼을 누른다. 이렇게 함으로써 광고주들은 중요한 사실을 알게 되는데, 가령 어떤 프로그램이 여성들에게 인기 있는지, 또는 어떤 연령대가 특정 프로그램을 가장 좋아하는지와 같은 것이다.

유감스럽게도, 이 시청률 수치들이 신뢰할 만한지에 관한 약간의 의구심이 있다. 일부 문제가 되는 것은 표본의 크기이다. 종합해서, 시청자층 조사에 이용되는 미국의 25,000세대는 전체 인구의 겨우 0.02%에 해당한다. 따라서 미국인 99.9%의 시청 습관은 무시되고 있는 것이다.

피플 미터에 관한 몇몇 특정 비판도 있다. 피플 미터는 방을 출입할 때 일관성 있게 버튼을 누르는 사람들에게 의존한다. 이 문제를 해결하기 위해 특별 카메라가 생겨났지만, 가격이 비싸 대부분의 세대에 설치되지 못했다. 게다가 사람들은 점점 자기 집이 아닌 곳, 가령 식당이나 기타 공공장소에서 TV를 시청한다. 그리고 물론, 인터넷과 스마트폰으로 프로그램을 시청하는 것이 점점 인기가 많아지는 것도 정확한 시청자층 조사에 전적으로 새로운 문제를 만들어 낸다.

구문 해설

14행 Nowadays, however, most TV meters have **been replaced with** "people meters."
▶ replace A with B(A를 B로 대체하다)가 수동태로 쓰임

26행 ..., but their high cost has **prevented** them **from being** installed in most households.
▶ prevent + 목적어 + from v-ing: ~가 …하지 못하도록 하다

27행 Furthermore, people increasingly watch TV in places **other than** their own home, ...
▶ other than: ~ 외에, ~이 아닌

UNIT 04.
Biology

READING 1
p. 22~23

WORD FOCUS   harmful
damaging 손해를 끼치는 / dangerous 위험한 / adverse 불리한, 해로운 / negative 부정적인

해석
아무도 삶을 혼자 살 수 없지만, 어떤 생물들은 다른 생물들보다 더 많이 삶을 함께한다. 자연에서 다른 종들 사이의 가장 가까운 관계는 공생이라 불린다. 그것은 '함께'와 '삶'을 의미하는 그리스어에서 형성된 이름이다. 과거에 '공생'이라는 용어는 두 생물 모두가 이득을 보는 관계에만 사용되었다. 하지만 오늘날 그것은 더 다양한 상호 작용을 나타낸다.

공생의 첫 번째 유형은 상리 공생이라 불리며, 그것은 그 단어의 원래 의미를 말한다. 상리 공생에서는 두 종 모두 그들의 상호 작용에서 무언가를 얻는다. 흰동가리와 말미잘이 좋은 예이다. 흰동가리는 말미잘의 쏘는 촉수 안에 산다. 그것들은 독침에 면역이 되어 있으며, 촉수는 그것들을 포식자로부터 보호해 준다. 보답으로, 흰동가리는 말미잘의 기생 동물을 잡아먹고, 다른 물고기를 말미잘의 사정권 안으로 유인한다.

공생의 두 번째 유형은 편리 공생이라 불린다. 이 상호 작용의 유형에서는 한 유기체가 득을 보는 데 반해 다른 유기체는 거의 영향을 받지 않는다. 빨판상어는 자신의 머리 위에 흡착기 같은 역할을 하는 기관이 달린 물고기이다. 그것들은 자신들을 상어를 포함한 더 큰 바다 생물에 달라붙게 하는 데 이 기관을 사용한다. 이것은 더 큰 동물에게 해가 되지 않는다. 물고기는 물에서 산소를 얻을 수 있도록 끊임없이 헤엄치거나 아가미를 움직여야 하지만, 빨판상어는 그것의 숙주 덕분에 자신의 힘을 소모하지 않고 물 속을 빠르게 이동할 수 있다.

공생의 세 번째 유형은 기생이라 불린다. 이러한 경우에는 관계에 있는 생물들 중 하나가 다른 생물에게 해를 끼침으로써 이득을 본다. 벼룩과 진드기가 너무나도 친숙한 예이다. 벼룩은 동물의 몸에 살면서 배가 고파지면 그것의 피를 빨아먹는다. 진드기도 동물의 피를 빨아먹기 위해 그것의 피부에 자신의 머리를 묻는다. 기생 동물은 끊임없이 먹이를 공급받음으로써 이익을 얻지만, 그것의 숙주는 고통받는다. 숙주에게서 영양분을 빼앗아가는 것 외에도, 이 기생 동물들은 치명적일 수 있는 많은 질병도 옮긴다.

공생 관계는 생물이 관계를 맺는 방식에 관한 대단히 흥미로운 예이다. 상리 공생과 편리 공생이 유일한 형태라면 좋겠지만, 기생은 불가피하며, 그것은 유기체가 살아남을 수 있는 어떤 방법이라도 찾을 것이라는 것을 보여준다.

구문 해설
5행 In the past, the term "symbiosis" was used only for relationships [in which both creatures benefit].

7

(25행) **Besides** taking nutrients away from the host, these parasites also carry <u>many diseases</u> [that can be deadly].

▶ Besides: ~ 외에도, ~에 더하여(전치사)

(28행) It **would be** nice if mutualism and commensalism **were** the only forms, ..., and it shows [*that* organisms will find any way possible to survive].

▶ 「If + S + 동사의 과거형, S + 조동사의 과거형 + 동사원형」은 '(만약) ~라면 …할 텐데'라는 의미의 가정법 과거

▶ 접속사 that 이하는 동사 shows의 목적어로 쓰임

READING 2   p. 24~25

WORD FOCUS   accomplish

fail 실패하다 / abandon 그만두다 / give up 포기하다

WORD CHECK

1. tissue   2. vulnerable   3. sprout   4. intense
5. dehydrate

▶ multitude: a large number of people or things

정답

1. a   2. ⓑ   3. d   4. By growing tall trunks with branches only near the top / By dropping their dead lower branches as they grow   5. d   6. unchanged, exposed, dehydrated, high, fuel

해석

들불은 지나는 길에 있는 모든 것을 태우면서 숲과 평야를 휩쓸고 지나간다. 동물과는 달리 식물에게는 불길로부터 달아날 방법이 없다. 하지만 그것들은 화재로부터 자신을 보호하기 위해 몇 가지 생존 전략을 개발해 왔다. 몇 가지 경우에 불은 심지어 그들의 생명 주기에 필요한 부분이다.

어떤 식물들은 불이 난 이후에만 싹이 트는 씨앗을 가지고 있다. 어떤 소나무는 송진이라 불리는, 접착제와 같은 물질로 봉해진 보호용 솔방울 안에서 씨앗을 키운다. 빠르게 번지는 불이 휩쓸고 지나가면, 송진이 녹고 결국 씨앗이 땅에 떨어져서 자라난다. 다른 식물들은 수년간 흙 속에서 변하지 않는 씨앗을 가지고 있다. 그 씨앗은 불이 흙 속에서 만들어 내는 극심한 열기나 화학 변화에 그것이 노출되고 나서야 자라게 해 주는 단단한 막을 가지고 있다.

두 번째 생존 전략은 불로부터 성체 식물의 살아있는 조직을 보호하는 것과 관련이 있다. 어떤 나무는 매우 타기 힘든 두꺼운 나무껍질을 가지고 있다. 그것은 나무가 불길에 둘러싸였을 때조차도 나무를 극심한 열기에서 안전하게 지켜준다. 이 전략의 다른 변형은 보호를 위해 촉촉한 조직을 자라게 하는 식물에서 찾을 수 있다. 화재 시에 그 습기가 식물들이 불에 타거나 건조해지는 것을 막아준다.

다른 경우에서, 화재 생존 전략은 식물의 취약한 부분이 불길에 닿지 않도록 하는 데 주력한다. 몇 종류의 나무가 가지가 꼭대기 근처에만 달린 높은 몸통을 자라게 함으로써 이것을 해낸다. 그것들 중 일부는 자라면서 더 낮은 곳에 있는 죽은 나뭇가지들을 떨어뜨리는데, 이는 꼭대기의 살아 있는 가지들이 불로부터 안전할 수 있게 해 준다. 이것은 중요한데, 죽은 나뭇가지가 나무 꼭대기의 살아 있는 꽃, 잎, 그리고 다른 중요한 조직 가까이에서 위험하게 타는 불길을 유지하게 하는 연료를 제공하기 때문이다.

식물계에는 다른 화재 방어 전략들도 존재한다. 예를 들어, 어떤 유칼립투스 종은 나무껍질 아래에, 불이 난 후에만 새로운 가지를 형성하는 새싹을 지닌 반면, 글로리오사는 불이 그것들로 하여금 빠르게 꽃을 피우게 할 때까지 꽃이 없는 상태로 있다. 불은 자연의 일부이며, 식물들은 불과 함께 살아갈 다수의 방법을 가지고 있다.

구문 해설

(1행) Wildfires sweep through forests and plains, **burning** everything in their path.

▶ burning 이하는 부대상황을 나타내는 분사구문

(8행) Certain pine trees grow their seeds inside of <u>protective cones</u> {sealed up with <u>a glue-like substance</u> [called resin]}.

(12행) The seeds have <u>tough coatings</u> {**that** do*n't* allow them to grow *until* they have been exposed to extreme heat or <u>the chemical changes</u> [**that** a fire produces ∧ in the soil]}.

▶ 첫 번째 that은 주격 관계대명사, 두 번째 that은 목적격 관계대명사

▶ not ~ until ...: …하고 나서야 (비로소) ~하다

WORD REVIEW TEST

UNIT 03   p. 26

1. d   2. c   3. d   4. c   5. c   6. a   7. d   8. b
9. share   10. track   11. households   12. statistics
13. rebuild   14. struggle   15. abandon   16. media

UNIT 04   p. 27

1. b   2. c   3. c   4. d   5. d   6. a   7. b   8. c
9. b   10. b   11. c   12. suffer   13. relationship
14. sweep   15. benefit

UNIT 05.
History

READING 1   p. 28~29

WORD FOCUS   complete

absolute 완전한, 온전한 / utter 완전한, 전적인 / thorough 완전한 / full 완전한, 전부의

WORD CHECK

1. govern   2. aggressive   3. treaty   4. controversy
5. indigenous

▶ establish: to start or create sth

정답

1. c   2. d   3. b   4. b, a, d   5. It was set up to help Māori tribes that had been mistreated.   6. settlers, treaty, Translation, established

해석

　뉴질랜드의 토착민인 마오리족은 13세기부터 그곳에 살았다. 1642년에 네덜란드인 탐험가가 그 섬들을 발견했고, 18세기에 유럽 이주민들이 도착하기 시작했다. 1840년쯤에는 그 섬에 약 2,000명의 이주민과 125,000명의 마오리족이 살고 있었다.

　점점 더 많은 이주민들이 도착하자, 마오리족의 지도자들은 걱정하기 시작했다. 그들은 영국에게 자신들의 땅을 빼앗으려 하는 영국 이주민들뿐만 아니라 프랑스와 같은 공격적인 나라들로부터의 보호를 요청했다. 영국 정부는 마오리족의 족장과 공식적인 조약을 체결하는 데 동의했는데, 그것은 영어로 쓰인 다음 마오리어로 번역되었다. 1840년에 그 조약은 영국과 43명의 족장에 의해 서명되었고 그 다음 8개월에 걸쳐 전국으로 수송되었는데, 그곳에서 그것은 500명이 넘는 마오리 족장들에 의해 서명되었다.

　와이탕이 조약은 세 개의 주요 조항으로 구성되어 있었다. 첫 번째는 영국 왕가에 뉴질랜드 전체의 주권을 이양했다. 두 번째는 족장들이 토지를 오직 영국 정부에게만 팔 수 있다는 것을 명시하면서, 그들이 그것을 계속 소유하는 것을 허용했다. 마지막으로, 그 조약은 모든 마오리족에게 영국 시민과 같은 권리를 주었다. 안타깝게도 곧 번역 문제가 논란을 일으켰다. 주된 문제는 '주권'이라는 단어에 관한 것이었는데, 그것은 '한 집단에 대해 완전한 권력을 가지는 것'을 의미했다. 하지만 그것은 '하나의 독립된 집단을 다스릴 권리'를 의미하는 마오리어로 번역되었다. 이 때문에, 영국은 그 조약이 그들에게 마오리족과 그들의 땅에 대한 완전한 권한을 주었다고 생각했다. 하지만 마오리족은 그 조약은 단순히 영국이 자신들의 땅을 사용하게 해 주는 것이라고 생각했다.

　이러한 의견 차이는 뉴질랜드 토지 전쟁으로 이어졌는데, 그것은 1845년부터 1872년까지 치러졌다. 양측에서 수백 명이 사망했으나, 결국 영국이 승리했다. 이것은 뉴질랜드의 거의 모든 토지가 영국에 귀속될 때까지 20세기에도 계속된 행위인 마오리족 토지의 몰수로 이어졌다.

　부당한 대우를 받았던 마오리 부족을 돕기 위해 1975년에 와이탕이 재판소가 설립되었다. 재판소가 조약의 조항들이 위배되었다는 판결을 내리면, 그 부족은 보상을 받는다. 비록 와이탕이 조약에 관한 논쟁이 오늘날 계속되고 있지만, 그것은 뉴질랜드 역사상 가장 중요한 문서 중 하나로 여겨진다.

구문 해설

[6행]   They asked Britain for protection *from aggressive countries*, such as France, **as well as** *from British settlers* [who tried to steal their land].

▶ A as well as B: 'B뿐만 아니라 A도'라는 뜻으로, 위 문장의 as well as는 from이 이끄는 두 개의 전치사구를 연결함

[14행]   The second **allowed** the chiefs **to keep** their land, *stating* [**that** they could sell it only to the British government].

▶ allow + 목적어 + to-v: ~이 …하도록 해 주다
▶ stating 이하는 부대상황을 나타내는 분사구문
▶ 접속사 that 이하는 stating의 목적어로 쓰임

[24행]   This led to the confiscation of Māori land, a practice [which continued into the 20th century], ...

READING 2   TOEFL   p. 30~31

정답

1. ⓒ   2. the fourth square   3. ⓒ   4. ⓑ   5. ⓒ
6. ⓑ, ⓔ, ⓕ

해석

미국 남북 전쟁

　1860년쯤에는 미국 북부와 남부의 주들이 대립된 경제적 · 정치적 견해를 가진 두 개의 다른 지역으로 발전했다. 정치적으로, 북부는 주들을 하나의 연합으로 통합시키는 중앙 정부를 필요로 한 반면, 남부는 주의 권한이 중앙 정부보다 더 중요하다고 여겼다. 북부와 남부는 특히 노예 제도 문제를 놓고 가장 첨예하게 갈라져 있었는데, 그 이유는 그들이 서로 다른 경제적 이해관계를 가지고 있었기 때문이었다. 즉, 남부는 노예 제도의 필요성에 대해 확고한 태도를 보인 반면, 북부는 강하게 노예 제도를 반대했다. 이런 의견의 불일치는 미국 남북 전쟁의 주된 이유가 되었는데, 그것은 1861년부터 1865년까지 지속되었다.

　남부에서는 인구의 겨우 5%를 차지하는 지주들이 면화, 담배, 사탕수수를 재배하기 위해 대농장을 경영했고, 농장을 유지하는 데 4백만 명이 넘는 노예들이 필수적이었다. 남부에서는 산업 혁명 기간 중 조면기(繰綿機)와 기타 기계들의 개발로 면화 농업이 급성장했다. 남부의 주들은 농작물을 재배해서 부를 축적했다. 그렇게 하기 위해서 그들은 노예들의 값싼 노동력에 의존했고, 따라서 노예제를 폐지하고자 하는 노력에 반대하였다. <u>한편, 북부는 산업 자본주의 사회로 발전했다. 섬유, 종이, 그리고 금속과 같</u>

은 공산품 생산이 증가함에 따라, 더는 농업에 의존하지 않게 되었다. 따라서, 북부 사람들은 노예제의 필요성을 거의 느끼지 못했고 그것에 반대할 가능성이 더 컸다.

이러한 배경에서 노예 제도를 반대하던 에이브러햄 링컨이 1861년에 대통령에 당선되었다. 남부의 일곱 개 주가 독립하고 그 해 말에 섬터 요새를 공격하며 미국 남북 전쟁의 시작을 알렸다. 1864년 7월까지 전쟁은 게티즈버그에서 승리를 거둔 북부에 유리하게 돌아가고 있었다. 전쟁은 결국 남군이 1865년에 항복하면서 종결되었다.

오랫동안 이어진 전쟁은 남부의 사회적·경제적 구조를 바꾸어 놓았다. 대규모 농장은 사라지고, 남부에 투자하기 위해 북부에서 자본가들이 떼지어 몰려오면서 석유, 석탄과 같은 자원뿐 아니라 섬유, 담배, 철 같은 산업의 급속한 성장을 가져왔다. 1869년과 1870년 사이 산업 생산 전체가 두 배로 증가하면서 미국 자본주의는 꽃을 피웠다.

구문 해설

23행 The drawn-out war **forced** social and economic structures of the South **to change**.
▶ force + 목적어 + to-v: ~로 하여금 (강제로) …하게 하다

26행 …, American capitalism bloomed, **with** industrial production *as a whole* **doubling**.
▶ with + 목적어 + v-ing: ~이 …한 채로
▶ as a whole: 전체적으로

UNIT 06.
People

READING 1
p. 32~33

WORD FOCUS   skilled

inexperienced 경험이 부족한 / clumsy 어설픈, 서투른 / incompetent 무능한

WORD CHECK

1. legacy   2. attachment   3. real estate
4. companion   5. amateur
▶ unspoiled: being pure and not damaged or changed

정답

1. c   2. ⓑ   3. b   4. She strived to preserve traditional lifestyles and farming methods.   5. b
6. (1) ⓑ (2) ⓒ (3) ⓓ (4) ⓐ

해석

작가 베아트릭스 포터는 숙련되고 영향력 있는 아마추어 생물학자이자 양을 치는 농부였으며, 자연 보호론자이기도 했지만, 1902년에 〈피터 래빗 이야기〉라는 아동용 책을 쓴 것으로 가장 유명하다. 벤자민 버니와 스쿼럴 너트킨처럼 그녀가 만들어낸 캐릭터들은 전 세계의 어린이들을 감동시켰고, (사람들이) 수백만 권의 책을 사게끔 했으며, 그녀의 다른 활동들이 남긴 유산은 오늘날에도 여전히 높이 평가될 만하다.

어린 시절, 그녀의 남동생이 교육을 받기 위해 외지로 보내진 반면, 베아트릭스는 집에서 여자 가정교사에 의해 교육을 받았다. 그녀는 자주 혼자 남겨졌고 자연 속에서 많은 시간을 보냈다. 이는 그녀가 동물들에 대해 강한 애착을 갖도록 만들었고, 그녀는 기회가 있을 때마다 그것들을 벗삼아 집으로 몰래 데려왔다. 동물들의 행동을 연구하면서 그녀는 그것들을 그리는 연습을 했고, 그것들에 대한 이야기를 만들어 냈다. 〈피터 래빗 이야기〉는 그녀의 예전 가정교사의 아들에게 쓴 편지에 기반을 두었고, 실제 토끼의 행동에서 영감을 받았다.

〈피터 래빗 이야기〉의 판매가 1년도 안 되어 5만 부를 넘자, 포터는 판매 수익을 부동산을 구입하는 데 쓰기 시작했다. 땅을 사들이는 데 있어 그녀의 목적은 아름답거나 역사적으로 중요한 땅과 건물을 보호하고 보존하기 위해서 설립된 기관인 내셔널 트러스트에 기증할 영국의 전원을 보존하기 위함이었다. 그녀는 땅을 샀을 뿐만 아니라 그것을 경작하기도 했다. 그녀는 경작하는 법을 배우면서 양을 키우는 일을 직업으로 삼기도 했다. 농부로 일하면서 베아트릭스는 전통적인 생활 방식과 농법이 잊혀지지 않게 하는 것을 목표로 했다.

1943년에 그녀가 삶을 마감했을 때, 베아트릭스 포터는 4,000 에이커의 땅이 그 아름다움을 잃지 않고 유지하도록 하기 위해 그것을 내셔널 트러스트에 남겼다. 그녀의 유산은 현재 레이크 디스트릭트 국립 공원의 일부가 되어, 다음 세대들을 위해 그녀가 쓴 작품들 속에 묘사된 자연의 아름다움에 대한 이미지뿐만 아니라 그녀의 책에 영감을 준 실제 장소들을 보존하는 데도 일조하고 있다.

구문 해설

15행 … to preserve the British countryside for the National Trust, an organization [set up … or historical importance].

20행 …, Beatrix Potter **left** 4,000 acres of land **to** the National Trust *to ensure* that its beauty could remain unspoiled.
▶ leave A to B: A를 B에게 남기다
▶ to ensure는 목적을 나타내는 부사적 용법의 to부정사

p. 34~35

WORD FOCUS set

set down ~을 적어 두다 / set free ~을 해방하다, 자유가 되게 하다 / set a standard 기준을 정하다 / set a limit 제한을 두다

WORD CHECK

1. anything but 2. commemorate 3. artificial
4. amputate 5. competitive

▶ insistence: an unending demand; a firm request

정답

1. a 2. d 3. Because his cancer (had) spread to his lungs and he was dying. 4. c 5. b 6. legacy, Diagnosed, funds, half

해석

그의 어머니 말씀을 듣는다면, 당신은 테리 폭스가 '매우 평범한 젊은 이'였다고 생각할 것이다. 그러나 그의 짧은 인생이 남긴 유산은 결코 평범하지 않다. 그는 두 편의 영화와 두 곡의 노래의 소재가 되었고, 그의 이름을 따서 이름이 지어진 산도 있으며, 한 동전의 앞면에도 그의 모습이 새겨져 있다.

장거리 육상 선수이자 농구 선수였던 테리는 18세의 나이에 골수암 진단을 받았다. 한쪽 다리를 무릎 위까지 절단하고 난 후에, 그가 목격한 다른 암 환자들의 고통은 그로 하여금 무엇인가를 해야 한다는 확신을 주었다. 그래서 그는 암 연구를 위한 기금을 모금해 보기로 했는데, 그 방법은 놀랍게도 캐나다를 횡단해서 달림으로써 단지 암이 다리 하나를 앗아갔다는 이유로 그가 더 열등한 사람인 것은 아니라는 것을 보여주는 것이었다. 1980년 4월 12일에 테리 폭스는 긴 여정을 시작했다. 세인트 존스에서 시작해, 그의 목표는 8,000km 이상 떨어진 밴쿠버까지 달려서, 캐나다 사람 1인당 1달러씩 해서 2천4백만 달러의 기부금을 모으는 것이었다.

원래 다리 한쪽과 의족 한쪽으로 여정을 시작한 폭스는 어떻게 해서든 하루에 42km, 즉 대략 마라톤 거리만큼을 달렸다. 143일 후 그는 캐나다 횡단이라는 목표를 달성하는 데 있어 절반 이상을 훨씬 넘겼지만, 그 날이 그가 마지막으로 달리는 날이 되고 말았다. 테리의 암은 폐까지 퍼져 있었고, 그는 '희망의 마라톤'을 완주하겠다는 꿈과 함께 죽어가고 있었다.

죽기 전에 그는 자신의 희망의 마라톤을 기념하기 위해 테리 폭스 달리기(Terry Fox Run)를 창설하는 것을 도왔다. 해마다 사람들은 기부금을 모으고 그를 기리는 단거리 마라톤을 뛰면서 암 연구를 위한 기금 모금에 도움을 주고 있다. 테리의 주장에 따라, 테리 폭스 달리기는 경쟁을 하지 않는다. 우승자도 없고 리본도 없으며 상도 없다. 오늘날 테리 폭스 달리기는 해마다 60개국이 넘는 곳에서 개최되고 있으며 암 연구를 위해 7억 5천만 달러 이상을 모금했다. 암 치료법에 대한 그의 희망은 그가 이룬 놀라운 업적에 끊임없이 영감을 받는 사람들 안에 계속 살아 있다.

구문 해설

1행 **If** you **were to** listen to his mother, you would think that ....

▶ 가정법 과거 문장에서 if절에 were to를 사용하여 미래에 실현 가능성이 희박한 일을 나타낼 수 있음

7행 After he **had** his leg **amputated** above the knee, ...

▶ have + 목적어 + p.p.: ~을 …되게 하다

WORD REVIEW TEST

UNIT 05 p. 36

1. c 2. b 3. b 4. b 5. a 6. d 7. c 8. a
9. d 10. a 11. b 12. compensation 13. burgeon
14. invest 15. sustainability

UNIT 06 p. 37

1. c 2. d 3. c 4. c 5. b 6. d 7. a
8. diagnosed 9. skilled 10. commemorate
11. exceed 12. ordinary 13. character
14. acquire 15. governess

UNIT 07.
Places

READING 1 p. 38~39

WORD FOCUS essential

unimportant 중요하지 않은 / optional 임의의 / unnecessary 불필요한 / irrelevant 무관한, 부적절한

WORD CHECK

1. cooperative 2. ensure 3. spectacle 4. expand
5. wilderness

▶ mystical: having qualities that are unreal or beyond what people can understand

정답

1. d 2. b 3. d 4. They provide important information on everything from the earth's ancient geological history to climate change. 5. b
6. extreme, aurora, horizon, research

지구의 가장 아름다운 자연환경들 중 많은 곳이 인간의 존재로 영향을 받아왔다. 하지만 호주 규모의 약 2배에 해당하는 남극 대륙은 상대적으로 본래 그대로의 신비한 땅으로 남아 있다. 이 최남단의 대륙은 여러 이유로 가치가 있다. 그곳은 훼손되지 않은 자연 그대로의 황무지, 대단한 아름다움, 그리고 중요한 과학 연구의 장소이다.

남극 대륙의 황무지는 숲이나 밀림의 것과는 다르다. 여러분은 그곳에서 어떤 식물도 찾을 수 없을 것이고, 동물도 거의 없다. 또한, 그곳은 극한의 땅으로 대륙 중에서 가장 춥고 건조하며, 평균 고도가 가장 높다. 대륙의 약 98%가 유럽 전체보다 더 큰 거대한 빙상으로 덮여 있다. 그리고 대륙에 겨우 몇천 명의 과학자들만 살고 있기 때문에, 남극 대륙은 거의 전적으로 자연 상태로 남아 있다.

게다가, 남극 대륙은 경이로운 아름다움으로도 소중히 여겨지고 있다. 그곳의 순백색의 땅은 지평선을 향해 끝없이 펼쳐져 있고, 밤에는 오로라라고 불리는 색이 있는 빛의 띠가 하늘에서 춤을 춘다. '극야'도 있는데, 그때에는 밤이 24시간 넘게 지속된다. 이 긴 밤 전후에, 태양은 지평선 위로 아주 조금 떠오른다. 그러고는 그것은 마치 땅을 따라서 천천히 굴러가는 것처럼 움직이며 아름답고 신비로운 장관을 연출한다.

남극은 또한 과학 연구 장소로 매우 가치가 있다. 1958년에 남극 조약이 남극 대륙을 평화적 · 협조적인 국제 연구 지역으로 설정하였다. 매년 27개국이 넘는 곳에서 온 1,000명에서 4,000명에 이르는 과학자들이 그곳의 연구소에서 생활하며 일한다. 그들이 행하는 실험은 지구의 고대 지질학적 역사에서부터 기후 변화에 이르는 모든 것에 대한 중요한 정보를 제공해 줌으로써, 우리가 지구를 더 잘 이해할 수 있도록 돕는다.

이러한 고유하고 독특한 특징들 때문에 모든 국가는 남극 대륙이 반드시 보호되고 보존될 수 있도록 협력해야 한다. 남극 대륙에서 일어나는 모든 활동은 환경에 최소한의 영향을 미쳐야 한다. 그렇게 함으로써, 남극 대륙은 앞으로 수년간 소중한 보물로 남을 수 있다.

구문 해설

9행 The wilderness of Antarctica is unlike **that** of a forest or jungle.
▶ that은 앞에 나온 단수명사 The wilderness의 반복을 피하기 위해 사용된 대명사

16행 ..., and at night, streamers of colored light, **called an aurora**, dance across the sky.
(S: streamers of colored light / V: dance)
▶ called an aurora는 주어에 대해 부연 설명하는 삽입절로, 콤마(,)를 사용해서 나타냄

19행 It then moves **as if it were rolling** slowly along the ground, ...
▶ as if + 가정법 과거: 마치 ~인 것처럼 (주절의 시제와 일치하되, 사실과 반대되는 일을 가정함)

WORD FOCUS   originate

begin 시작하다 / emerge 생겨나다 / arise 생기다, 발생하다

WORD CHECK

1. evaporate   2. accessible   3. lava   4. fertile
5. extreme
▶ livelihood: a way of earning money to buy what you need

정답

1. a   2. c   3. It confirmed that humans originated in Africa.   4. d   5. (1) F (2) T (3) F   6. (1) ⓒ (2) ⓐ (3) ⓓ (4) ⓑ (5) ⓔ

해석

때때로 '지옥으로 가는 관문'이라 불리기도 하는 장소에서, 밤에는 용암 웅덩이가 빛나고 낮 동안에는 건조된 소금의 눈부신 하얀 막 위에서 신기루가 춤을 춘다. 이곳은 지구상에서 가장 뜨거운 곳 중 하나인 다나킬 함몰지이다. 그곳은 에티오피아 북동부 지역의 약 100,000 평방 킬로미터에 걸쳐져 있다.

다나킬 함몰지는 지구의 지질 구조 판이 떨어져 이동하고 새로운 지각이 형성되는 장소인 열곡의 일부인데, 그것은 그 지역이 지질학적으로 매우 활발하다는 것을 의미한다. 그곳에는 화산, 온천, 그리고 유황과 다른 광물로 가득한 형형색색의 웅덩이가 있다. 지구 내부로부터 나오는 열은 극한 기온의 원인이 되는데, 여름에 그것은 섭씨 55도에 이른다. 예전에는 전 지역이 홍해의 일부였지만, 용암의 축적이 그것을 내륙해로 분리시켰다. 후에, 그 물은 건조한 기후에 증발하여 광대한 소금 퇴적물을 남겼다.

살기 힘든 기후임에도 불구하고, 다나킬 함몰지는 생명체의 진화를 연구하는 데 도움이 되어 왔다. 가장 오래된 것으로 알려진 초기 인류 조상의 화석 중 하나인 루시가 1974년에 이곳에서 발견되어 인류가 아프리카에서 기원했음을 확인해 주었다. 게다가, 그 지역의 온천들은 지구의 과거나 다른 행성의 극한의 환경과 유사할지도 모르는 환경에서 사는 고대 미생물 종의 서식지이다.

현대 인류는 다나킬 함몰지에서 생존할 방법을 찾아냈다. 아파르인들은 이동식 목조 오두막에서 지내고 동물들을 몰면서 그 지역을 돌아다닌다. 아와시 강은 그들에게 물과, 그들의 동물들이 풀을 뜯을 수 있는 약간의 비옥한 땅을 제공해 준다. 그들의 생계는 소금 장사에 기반한다. 그들은 도시에서 소금 덩어리를 팔기 위해 그것들을 잘라내고, 낙타와 당나귀에 실어 일주일 동안 걷는다. 그들의 몸이 열에 적응했기 때문에, 그들은 약간의 빵과 물만을 가지고 이 여정에서 살아남을 수 있다.

결국 홍해가 아마 다나킬 함몰지를 다시 덮겠지만, 수백만 년 동안은 그러지 않을 것이다. 지금 그곳은 다른 행성의 생명체에 대한 단서를 줄 수도 있는 생물 형태에 매료된 과학자들과, 그곳에 살며 생계를 유지하는 사람들이 이용할 수 있는 곳으로 남아 있다.

[5행] The Danakil Depression is part of a rift valley, a

place [where the earth's tectonic plates are moving

apart and new crust is forming], ...

[10행] ...; later, the water evaporated in the dry climate,

leaving vast deposits of salt.

▶ leaving 이하는 결과를 나타내는 분사구문

[15행] ... are home to ancient species of microbes {that live

in extreme conditions [that may be similar to **those**

from earth's past or on other planets]}.

▶ those는 앞에 나온 복수명사 extreme conditions의 반복
을 피하기 위해 사용된 대명사

UNIT 08.
Economy

READING 1   p. 42~43

WORD FOCUS burden

bear a burden 부담을 지다 / ease a burden 부담을 줄이다 /
a debt burden 부채 부담 / a tax burden 조세 부담

WORD CHECK

1. shortage   2. shift   3. life span   4. boost   5. ratio
▶ outcome: sth that follows as a result

정답

1. a   2. c   3. It is the economic activities of senior
citizens.   4. d   5. d   6. percentage, taxes, shortage,
spend, opportunities

해석

2015년에, 세계 인구는 50세 이상의 16억 명이 넘는 사람을 포함했
다. 이 연령대는 과거에 그랬던 것보다 이미 더 많은 인구 비율을 차지하고
있으며, 전문가들은 2050년까지 그 수가 두 배가 될 것이라고 예측한다.
이 변화가 모든 곳의 경제를 바꾸고 있다.

어떤 이들은 이 변화를 부정적인 전개로 본다. 노인에 대한 청년의 비
율이 낮아지면서 노인들을 부양하기 위한 세금이 젊은 노동자들에게 더 부
담이 될 수도 있다. 더 많은 사람들이 사회 보장 제도에서 돈을 가져가는 데
반해, 더 적은 사람들이 그것에 돈을 불입하고 있다. 유럽에서는 현재 많은
국가들이 이것을 보완하기 위해 임금에 20% 이상의 세금을 부과한다. 노
년 인구의 의료 수요를 충족시키기 위해 더 많은 정부의 재원이 의료 서비

스에 쓰여야 하는데, 그것은 다른 곳에 더 적은 재원을 이용할 수 있다는 것
을 의미할 수도 있다. 게다가, 노인의 수가 증가하면서 그들을 돌볼 수 있도
록 교육받은 능숙한 근로자들이 부족하게 될 것이다. 이러한 어려움들은 많
은 사람들이 세계 경제의 미래에 대해 불안감을 느끼게 한다.

하지만 다른 이들은 인구 고령화의 경제적인 영향을 보다 긍정적으로
보고 있다. 일반적으로, 이 연령대는 국가의 재정 성장에 크게 기여한다. 노
인들의 경제 활동은 장수 경제라고 불리며, 그것은 의료 서비스에 대한 공
공 지출의 증가를 벌충할 수 있을 것이다. 예를 들어, 옥스포드 이코노믹스
는 50세 이상의 사람들이 미국 인구의 35%를 차지하지만, 국가 GDP의
43%를 생산하며 소비재에 지출되는 비용의 55%를 제공한다는 것을 밝혀
냈다. 노인은 젊은 사람들보다 더 높은 비율로 자원봉사를 하고 자선 단체
에 기부하며, 그들 중 많은 수가 작은 사업을 운영하여 다른 사람들을 위한
일자리를 창출한다. 장수 경제가 모두에게 득이 되는 경제 성장을 추진하기
때문에 인구 고령화는 실제로 수지가 맞을 수도 있다.

길어진 수명은 더 많은 의료 서비스의 필요성을 만들어 내어 젊은 납
세자에게 부담을 지우지만, 그것은 또한 사람들이 더 오랫동안 생산적으로
일할 수 있다는 것을 의미하는데, 이는 경기를 부양한다. 결과에 대한 의
견 차이는 계속되고, 세계는 긍정적인 것이 승리할지 부정적인 것이 승리
할지 지켜본다.

구문 해설

[8행] ..., taxes [intended to support **the elderly**] could

become more burdensome to young workers.

▶ the + 형용사: ~한 사람들

[11행] ..., more government resources must go towards

health care, **which** could mean [(*that*) fewer

resources are available elsewhere].

▶ which는 앞 절을 선행사로 하는 계속적 용법의 관계대명사

▶ fewer resources ... elsewhere는 동사 mean의 목적어로
쓰인 명사절로 fewer resources 앞에 접속사 that이 생략됨

READING 2   p. 44~45

WORD FOCUS superior

inferior ~보다 못한 / low-grade 질 낮은 / substandard 수준
이하의

WORD CHECK

1. constantly   2. advertise   3. accompany
4. convince   5. strategy
▶ annual: yearly; happening once per year

1. b   2. Let people try something once and make them become regular customers. / Give consumers something for free and make them purchase something to accompany it.   3. c   4. d   5. b   6. free, accompanying, popularized, upgrade

해석

　모든 사람이 공짜로 뭔가를 얻는 것을 좋아하며, 요즘은 갖가지 공짜 물건을 받는 것이 어느 때보다 쉽다. 기업들은 공짜 음식, 공짜 티셔츠, 심지어 공짜 휴대 전화까지 나누어 준다. 기업이 이런 일을 하는 것은 현명한 일이 아닌 것처럼 보일지도 모르지만, 실은 이것은 '프리코노믹스'라고 불리는 것에 기반한 잘 계획된 전략이다.

　프리코노믹스의 기본적인 한 가지 전략은 사람들을 단골 고객으로 만들기 위해 뭔가를 한 번 써 보게 하는 것이다. 예를 들어, 당신이 어느 날 아침 카페에서 공짜 커피를 받는다면, 당신은 똑같은 음료를 사기 위해 날마다 올지도 모른다. 이는 기업에서 당신에게 우편으로 작은 샴푸 용기를 보내는 것과 같은 이유이다. 그들은 당신이 다음번에 쇼핑을 갈 때는 큰 병을 구입하기를 바라는 것이다. 프리코노믹스의 또 다른 전략은 소비자들이 그 후에 그것에 수반되는 뭔가를 구매해야 할 것이라는 것을 알면서, 그들에게 무언가를 공짜로 주는 것이다. 예를 들어, 전화 회사에서 당신에게 공짜 휴대 전화를 줄지도 모르지만, 그러고 나면 당신은 연간 요금제를 지불해야 한다.

　프리코노믹스라는 개념은 한동안 존재해 왔지만, 인터넷이 그것을 그 어느 때보다 더 대중화시켰다. 인터넷 업체를 운영하는 비용이 매우 적기 때문에, 웹 사이트들은 더 많은 방문객을 끌어들이기를 바라고 끊임없이 무료 혜택을 제공하고 있다. 일부 사람들은 단지 무료 제공품을 이용할 것임에도 불구하고, 업체는 그들에게 좀 더 매력적인 유료 서비스로 상향 조정하라고 설득할 수 있을지도 모른다. 이것은 'freemium' 전략이라고 알려진 것으로, 'free(공짜의)'와 'premium(고급의)'이란 단어가 결합한 것이다.

　일부 전문가들은 프리코노믹스가 결국은 사업이 이루어지는 방식을 바꿀 것이라고 생각한다. 이미, 뛰어난 제품을 보유한 어떤 기업이든 잠재 고객에게 무료 체험을 하게 해주어 이득을 얻을 수 있다. 그리고 인터넷상에는 유튜브나 구글처럼 소비자들에게 어떤 것도 전혀 판매할 필요가 없는 사업체들이 많다. 그들은 단지 무료 서비스로 자신들의 웹 사이트에 수백만 명을 끌어들이고, 다른 업체가 그들의 사이트에서 광고를 하는 것에 대해 요금을 청구하는 것으로 이윤을 얻는다. 이러한 업체들은 수익을 얻고, 우리는 뭔가를 공짜로 즐길 수 있게 된다.

구문 해설

3행　..., but it's actually a well-planned strategy {based on something [called "freeconomics."]}

7행　This is the same reason [(**why**) a company might ... in the mail] ....
　▶ 선행사 the same reason 뒤에 관계부사 why가 생략됨

9행　Another strategy of freeconomics is to give consumers something for free, **knowing** they will then need to purchase something to accompany *it*.
　▶ knowing 이하는 동시동작을 나타내는 분사구문
　▶ it은 첫 번째 something을 가리킴

WORD REVIEW TEST

UNIT 07	p. 46

1. d   2. d   3. b   4. d   5. b   6. a   7. c
8. evaporates   9. continents   10. fertile
11. inhale   12. flexible   13. inhospitable
14. untouched   15. separate

UNIT 08	p. 47

1. d   2. b   3. c   4. c   5. a   6. b   7. b   8. d
9. a   10. b   11. superior   12. transform
13. predict   14. combination

UNIT 09.
Language

READING 1	p. 48~49

WORD FOCUS　entire
whole 전체의 / complete 전부의 / total 전체의 / full 완전한, 모든

WORD CHECK
1. extinction   2. simplify   3. distinctive
4. represent   5. widespread
▶ originate: to start or begin from somewhere

정답

1. d   2. Because in these surroundings, whistling can be heard more clearly and from farther away than shouting can.   3. b   4. d   5. d   6. (1) ⓒ (2) ⓐ (3) ⓑ (4) ⓓ

해석

휘파람을 부는 것은 흔히 생각 없이 하는 단순한 행동으로 여겨지지만, 어떤 사람들은 모든 대화를 하는 데 휘파람을 사용한다. 오늘날 70개나 되는 휘파람 언어가 전 세계적으로 사용된다. 어떤 것들은 스페인어와 같이 널리 사용되는 구어를 기반으로 하는 데 반해, 다른 것들은 사용자가 거의 없는 언어를 기반으로 한다. 보통 휘파람 언어들이 가지고 있는 공통점은 그것들이 산악 지대나 울창한 숲에서 사용된다는 것이다. 이러한 환경에서 휘파람은 소리를 지르는 것보다 더 분명하게, 더 멀리서도 들릴 수 있다.

휘파람 언어는 고립된 장소에서 사용되는 경향이 있어서 소멸될 위기에 처해 있다. 그리스 안티아의 휘파람 언어인 스피리아를 예로 들어 보자. 그것의 휘파람 소리는 그리스어의 구어음을 기반으로 한다. 휘파람 음조의 다양한 조합은 모음을 나타내고, 자음은 모음의 음조를 바꿈으로써 다시 만들어진다. 스피리아가 생겨난 마을에서는 인구가 37명으로 줄어들었다. 어떤 주민들은 노년기에 이가 빠져서, 그 (휘파람) 언어를 불 수 있는 사람은 단 6명만 남아 있다. 스피리아를 보존하기 위해 안티아 사람들은 외부인들에게 그것을 가르치는 데 동의했는데, 그것은 역사적으로 행해지지 않은 것이었으며, 2012년에 그들은 그리스로부터, 그리고 국제적으로 이목을 끈 축제를 열었다.

어떤 집단은 자신들의 휘파람 언어를 보존하는 데 꽤 성공했다. 북아프리카 부근에 있는 라고메라 섬에서, 실보 고메로라고 불리는 휘파람 언어는 사람들이 먼 거리에서도 스페인어로 소통할 수 있게 해 준다. 그것은 스페인어 소리를 두 개의 휘파람 모음과 네 개의 휘파람 자음으로 단순화함으로써 행해진다. 1950년대에는 새로운 통신 기술로 인해 실보 고메로의 사용이 감소했지만, 1980년대에 사람들은 그들이 잃어가던 것을 깨닫기 시작했고, 그것을 지키기 위한 조치를 취했다. 그들은 학교 수업을 부활시켰고 성인을 위한 프로그램을 도입해서, 오늘날 그 섬에 사는 남녀노소의 사람들이 실보 고메로를 사용할 수 있다.

우리에게는 장거리 통신 수단이 있는데 왜 (그들은) 휘파람 언어를 보존하기 위해 노력할까? 각각의 언어는 그것을 사용하는 사람들의 문화와 역사에 대한 정보를 전달한다. 모든 곳에 있는 사람들이 비슷한 방식으로 소통하기 시작한다면, 우리는 자신들만의 독특한 방식으로 세계를 보고 그것에 대해 말했던 사람들의 특별한 이야기들을 기억하게 될까?

구문 해설

16행 In an attempt to save Sfyria, the people of Antia agreed to teach it to outsiders, something [that was not done historically], ...

20행 ..., a whistled language [called Silbo Gomero] **allows** people **to communicate** in Spanish over long distances.
▶ allow + 목적어 + to-v: ~이 …하도록 해 주다

23행 ..., but in the 1980s, people **began** to realize *what* they were losing **and took** steps to protect it.
▶ 등위접속사 and로 동사 began과 took이 대등하게 연결됨
▶ what은 선행사를 포함하는 관계대명사로, '~하는 것'의 의미

READING 2 p. 50~51

WORD CHECK
1. ambition 2. foster 3. auxiliary 4. criticize
5. ethnic
▶ strife: difficulty, hardship, and pain caused by struggling

정답
1. b 2. b 3. c 4. It has vocabulary and grammar that are too closely related to Western European languages. / It has no culture. 5. a 6. (1) ⓓ (2) ⓐ (3) ⓑ (4) ⓒ

해석

만일 모든 사람이 한 가지 언어로 의사소통할 수 있다면 세상은 어떤 모습일까? 이 생각을 실행에 옮기려고 했던 한 사람이 있다. 바로 폴란드의 루도빅 라자루스 자멘호프 박사이다. 1870년대 후반에서 1880년대 초반에 걸쳐 개발된 그의 언어는 에스페란토라고 알려져 있다. 그것은 서로 다른 모국어를 구사하는 사람들 간에 사용하도록 만들어진 인공어이다. '에스페란토'라는 단어는 '희망하는 사람'이라는 뜻이다.

자멘호프의 목표는 평화와 국제적 이해를 증진하고, 분쟁과 갈등으로 이어지는 많은 문제를 해결하기 위해 쉽고도 융통성 있는 언어를 만들어 내는 것이었다. 그것은 민족어들을 대체하기 위함이 아니라 국제적 보조 언어, 즉 전 세계적인 제2언어의 역할을 하기 위함이었다. 이 언어를 사용하는 사람의 수는 이후 몇십 년 동안 급속도로 증가했는데, 처음에는 러시아 제국과 동유럽에서 주로 쓰이다가, 그다음에는 서유럽과 동아시아에서 쓰였다.

다른 언어들에 비해 에스페란토를 배우기 쉽게 만드는 세 가지 특별한 특징들이 있다. 우선, 이 언어의 체계가 한 가지 소리에 한 글자를 사용한다는 점인데, 그것은 구어와 문어를 아주 빨리 배우고 적용할 수 있다는 것을 의미한다. 게다가 에스페란토의 거의 모든 문법을 이해하기 위해서는 단 16개의 문법 규칙만 배우면 된다. 마지막으로, 가장 기본이 되는 어근으로부터 단어들을 만드는 것이 쉽고, 자신만의 단어를 만들어 내는 것도 허용된다.

약 2백만 명이 현재 에스페란토를 사용할 수 있는 것으로 추정된다. 하지만, 배우기 쉬운 체계에도 불구하고 에스페란토는 어떤 나라의 공식 언어도 되지 못했다. 이는 에스페란토가 서유럽의 언어들과 너무 밀접하게 연관된 어휘와 문법을 가지고 있다는 비판을 자주 받는 것 때문일 수 있다. 이 언어에 대한 또 하나의 일반적인 비판은 이 언어에 문화가 없다는 것이다. 그렇지만 에스페란토는 의도적으로 문화적 중립성을 지키고 있다. 이 언어는 문화 간의 조력자 역할을 하게끔 의도된 것이지, 어떤 한 문화의 운반자 역할을 하도록 의도된 것은 아니었다. 어쩌면 이 언어의 미래는 에스페란토를 사용하는 집단 내에 존재하는 양측 논쟁의 결과에 달려있다고 볼 수 있다. 즉, 에스페란토가 세계 제2언어가 되어야 한다는 원래의 목표를 지닌 측과, 큰 야심 없이 에스페란토를 일종의 대안적인 생활 양식으로 여기는 또 다른 측을 말한다.

15

구문 해설

8행 Zamenhof's goal was **to create** an easy and flexible

language ┌ *to foster* ... understanding

         │ and

         └ *to resolve* many ....

▶ to create는 문장의 주격보어로 쓰인 명사적 용법의 to부정사
이고, to foster와 to resolve는 목적을 나타내는 부사적 용법의
to부정사

14행 There are three particular features [that make

Esperanto easy to learn **compared to** other

languages].

▶ compared to: ~와 비교해서

UNIT 10.
Art

READING 1   p. 52~53

WORD CHECK

1. rank   2. insight   3. command   4. reproduction
5. remarkable

▶ foreground: the part of a scene in a picture that is meant
to seem nearest to the viewer

정답

1. c   2. It is famous for his command of light and
dark, often using contrast to draw the viewer into the
painting.   3. b   4. b   5. d   6. nature, depth, pain,
consistent

해석

바로크 시대의 화가인 렘브란트는 서양사에서 가장 위대한 화가 중 한
사람으로 손꼽힌다. 렘브란트 하르먼스존 판 레인은 1606년 7월 15일 네
덜란드의 레이던에서 태어났다. 그는 인간 본성에 대한 깊은 이해와 뛰어
난 기교를 결합하며 거의 600점에 이르는 그림을 그렸다. 렘브란트의 작품
은 명암 표현 능력으로 유명한데, 보는 사람을 그림 속으로 끌어들이는 (명
암) 대비를 자주 사용하였다. 이러한 특징은 그의 가장 큰 그림인 〈야간 순
찰〉에서 가장 잘 나타난다. 그것은 네덜란드 황금시대의 절정이었던 1642
년에 완성되었다.

그 그림을 직접 보면 명암의 극단적인 대비에 탄복하게 되는데, 그것은
동적 효과와 깊이감을 더한다. 그림의 전경에 거의 삼차원처럼 보이는 투창
을 들고 있는 한 남자가 있다. 이러한 착각을 일으키는 깊이감은 렘브란트
가 얼마나 천재였는지를 보여준다. 직선 원근법과 함께, 빛과 색을 사용하

는 그의 능력은 그의 그림에 활기를 불어넣는다. 하지만, 여러분이 책에서
〈야간 순찰〉의 복제본을 본다면 이를 감상할 수 없을 것이다. 직접 보면 정
말 실제 같은 투창이 사진에서는 전혀 두드러져 보이지 않는다.

1630년대 후반부터 렘브란트는 풍경화를 그리기 시작했다. 이 작품들
은 폭풍을 맞고 쓰러진 거대한 나무나 험상궂은 하늘과 같이 신비로운 장
면들을 보여주면서, 자연의 더 어두운 면에 중점을 두었다. 이러한 특징들
은 그의 그림인 〈폭풍우 몰아치는 풍경〉(1638)에서 찾아볼 수 있다. 그의
인생 막바지에 이르러, 렘브란트는 자신의 얼굴에 서려 있던 고뇌와 슬픔
의 느낌을 강조하여 그의 가장 훌륭한 자화상들 중 일부를 그렸다. 그것들
은 대중에게 알려진 그의 성공적인 이력과는 대조되는 그의 가슴 아픈 가
정사를 반영한 것이었다. 렘브란트가 그린 수많은 자화상들은 그 자신의 성
격 변화와 더불어 자신의 얼굴 이목구비가 노화되어 가는 과정의 두드러진
기록을 우리에게 보여준다.

당대의 다른 화가에 비해 렘브란트는 더 명료하게, 더 깊은 통찰력으
로 그를 둘러싼 세계를 연구했다. 그의 작품들을 통틀어 한결같이 지킨 높
은 기준은 그가 네덜란드 미술의 황금시대의 한 중심 인물이 되는 명성을
얻도록 해 주었다.

구문 해설

4행 **Combining** a deep understanding ... *with* brilliant
technique, he produced nearly 600 paintings.

▶ Combining ... technique은 부대상황을 나타내는 분사구문
▶ combine A with B: A와 B를 결합하다

12행 **Viewing** the painting in person, one is struck by ....

▶ Viewing ... in person은 조건을 나타내는 분사구문 (= If
one views the painting in person)

23행 They reflected his painful family life **as opposed to**
his successful public career.

▶ as opposed to: ~와는 대조적으로, ~와는 다르게

READING 2   TOEFL   p. 54~55

정답

1. ⓐ   2. ⓓ   3. the second square   4. ⓓ   5. ⓑ
6. ⓐ, ⓓ, ⓔ

해석

바로크 미술

르네상스 시대가 끝난 뒤, 유럽의 미술은 1600년경 바로크 시대의 도
래와 함께 변화를 겪었다. 바로크 양식은 로마에서 시작되어 유럽 대부분의
지역으로 퍼져 나갔다. 바로크 운동의 인기와 성공은 가톨릭 교회의 대중주
의 운동에 의해 장려되었다.

17세기에 있었던 종교 개혁의 도전에 대응하여 가톨릭 교회는 영성의
전통적인 가치를 장려했다. 가톨릭 교회는 교육을 받은 사람들뿐만 아니라
글을 모르는 사람들에게도 그 가르침을 전하기 위한 수단으로 미술을 이용
하려 했다. 다수의 바로크 미술가들은 직접적이고 감정적으로 개입해서 종

교적인 주제를 그렸다.

르네상스 시대의 고전 미술이 인간의 이성을 장려한 데 반해, 바로크 미술은 감정과 인간의 감성에 초점을 맞췄다. 감각에 호소하기 위한 하나의 시도로, 바로크 미술가들은 그들의 작품 속에서 감정과 다양성, 그리고 움직임을 보여주려고 했다. 그들은 명암의 강한 대비를 사용해서 이를 해냈다. 다양한 색을 사용하여 그들은 그림을 보다 더 감성적인 방식으로 보여주기 위해 명암의 힘을 강조했다. 그들은 또한 르네상스 시대에 쓰였던 것과 같이 이상화되고 완벽한 체형을 가진 모델 대신 실생활과 보통 사람들을 소재로 다루었다. 카라바조와 안니발레 카라치는 바로크 전통의 위대한 두 인물로, 이탈리아 미술에 새로운 풍부함을 가져왔다. 바로크 미술의 정점은 지안 로렌조 베르니니의 작품이었는데, 그는 힘이 넘치고 웅장한 예술 형식으로 바로크 시대 전성기를 주도했다.

바로크 운동은 사실상 로마에서 시작되었지만, 그것이 전파된 각 나라에서 어느 정도의 변화를 겪으면서, 결국 네덜란드, 프랑스, 독일, 그리고 스페인의 미술가들에게 영향을 미쳤다. 네덜란드의 바로크 양식은 일상생활에 좀 더 기반을 두었고, 베르메르와 렘브란트의 작품에서 나타나듯이 초상화, 풍경화, 그리고 정물화의 우세로 이어졌다. 프랑스에서는 바로크 양식이 주된 예술 형식으로 쓰였으며 군주제에 의해 장려되었다.

18세기가 시작될 즈음에, 바로크 양식은 파리의 미술계에서 발달한 좀 더 경쾌한 로코코 운동에 의해 대부분 대체되었다. 그럼에도 불구하고, 바로크 미술과 그 영향력은 계속해서 전 세계로 퍼져 나갔다.

구문 해설

13행 ... rather than idealized, perfectly formed models like **those** [used in the Renaissance period].
▶ those는 앞에 나온 복수명사 models의 반복을 피하기 위해 사용된 대명사

18행 Although the Baroque movement actually started in Rome, it eventually influenced ..., and Spain, **undergoing** some change ... to which it migrated.
▶ undergoing 이하는 부대상황을 나타내는 분사구문

WORD REVIEW TEST

1. c   2. d   3. a   4. b   5. c   6. d   7. b   8. a
9. extinction   10. revive   11. intentionally
12. estimated   13. 3   14. 2

UNIT 10
p. 57

1. b   2. c   3. c   4. d   5. b   6. a   7. c   8. d
9. c   10. b   11. grief   12. brilliant   13. illiterate
14. monarchy

UNIT 11.
Biotechnology

READING 1   p. 58~59

WORD FOCUS   harsh

comfortable 편안한, 쾌적한 / mild 온화한, 포근한 / gentle 부드러운, 온화한 / hospitable 쾌적한

WORD CHECK

1. microbe   2. innovative   3. inspiration
4. challenging   5. application
▶ metabolism: the process of breaking down and using energy in the body

정답

1. a   2. Nature has been undergoing a process of trial and error for billions of years.   3. c   4. b   5. b
6. inspiration, perfected, waterproof, resource

해석

인간은 끝없이 혁신적이다. 수 세기에 걸쳐 우리는 역사상 가장 어려운 문제들 중 일부를 해결하기 위해 많은 놀라운 생각과 발명품을 창조해 왔다. 하지만 이런 생각과 발명품 중 많은 것들의 영감은 자연으로부터 온 것이다. 심지어 이 분야를 나타내는 생체 모방 기술이라는 이름도 존재한다.

생체 모방 기술은 자연이 수십억 년 동안 시행착오 과정을 거쳐오고 있다는 사실을 이용한다. 그 시간 동안 자연은 식물과 동물이 어려운 상황과 거친 환경 속에서 살아남을 수 있게 하는 여러 체계와 과정을 완벽하게 만들었다. 따라서 역사를 통틀어 인간은 문제에 대한 해결책과 발명품을 위한 아이디어를 얻기 위해 자연을 관찰하고 있다. 예를 들어, 새의 몸은 비행기 디자인에 영감을 준 반면, 연꽃의 방수 특성은 방수 페인트를 제작하기 위해 모방되었다.

오늘날, 여러 새롭고 흥미로운 생체 모방 기술의 적용이 과학자들에 의해 고려되고 있다. 예를 들어, 거미가 거미줄을 만드는 데 사용되는 강한 실은 다리의 케이블을 만들기 위해 사용될 수 있는 탄력적인 물질로 공학자들을 이끌 수 있을 것이다. 과학자들은 물속 깊이 잠수하는 동물들이 뇌의 온도를 어떻게 낮추고, 신진대사를 어떻게 늦추는지를 알기 위해 그 동물들도 면밀히 연구해 오고 있다. 이는 의사들이 심각한 부상을 입은 환자의 몸을 비슷한 상태에 둠으로써 그들을 치료하는 방법을 찾는 데 도움이 될 수 있을 것으로 기대된다.

또한, 생체 모방 기술 연구는 매우 다양한 아이디어로도 행해지고 있다. 한 가지 설득력 있는 예는 식물의 잎이 새로운 종류의 태양 전지판 모델로 사용될 수 있는 방법에 관한 연구이다. 홍합이 자신을 바위에 부착시키기 위해 사용하는 물질은 외과 전문의들을 위한 무독성 접착제를 고안할 수 있도록 마찬가지로 연구되고 모방되고 있다. 궁극적으로, 생체 모방 기술은 인간과 자연 간의 새로운 종류의 관계를 만드는 것이다. 동물, 식물 및 미생

물을 통제하고 채취하는 자원으로 다루는 대신, 이제 우리는 그것들을 소중한 정보를 공유하는 스승으로 보고 있다.

구문 해설

8행 Biomimetics takes advantage of the fact **that** nature has been undergoing a process ... of years.
▶ that이 이끄는 절은 the fact와 동격 관계

17행 Scientists have also been carefully studying animals [that dive deep into the water] to learn **how** they *lower* their brain temperatures *and slow* their metabolisms.
▶ how가 이끄는 절은 learn의 목적어로 쓰인 간접의문문으로 「의문사 + 주어 + 동사」의 어순
▶ 등위접속사 and로 동사 lower와 slow가 대등하게 연결됨

23행 A substance [(**that**[**which**]) mussels use ∧ to attach themselves to rocks] is similarly being studied and copied ....
▶ mussels 앞에 A substance를 선행사로 하는 목적격 관계대명사가 생략됨
▶ to attach는 목적을 나타내는 부사적 용법의 to부정사

READING 2 　　　　　　　　p. 60~61

WORD FOCUS dim
bright 밝은 / brilliant 눈부신 / distinct 뚜렷한 / clear 뚜렷한

WORD CHECK
1. alert　2. phenomenon　3. generate　4. organism
5. detect
▶ glow: to produce a soft, steady light

정답
1. a　2. b　3. It produces almost no heat.　4. c
5. b　6. interacts, heat, eco-friendly, medical

해석

　거의 200년 전에, 찰스 다윈은 아주 작은 생물 발광의 유기체로 가득한 바닷물을 처음으로 관찰했던 때를 묘사했다. 그는 바다가 깜빡이는 빛으로 빛나고 있다고 적었다. 그는 또한 그 물이 병 속에 들어간 후에도 여전히 섬광을 내며 번쩍였다고 써두었다. 그 당시에는 무엇이 그 불빛을 생겨나게 했는지 아무도 몰랐지만, 그때부터 생물 발광은 많은 연구의 주제가 되어 왔다.

　생물 발광은 단순히 생명체에 의해 만들어진 빛을 의미한다. 반딧불이가 흔한 예이지만, 그 현상은 일부 어류, 버섯, 박테리아, 그리고 다른 생물에서도 발견된다. 이제 우리는 그 빛이 루시페린이라 불리는 화학 물질에 의해 만들어진다는 것을 안다. 유기체들은 루시페라아제라고 불리는 효소가 루시페린과 상호 작용할 때 빛이 나고, 여러 생물 속의 다양한 루시페린은 다른 색의 빛을 만들어 낸다.

　과거에 인간은 가끔 생물 발광을 이용했다. 나무에서 자라는 발광 곰팡이는 숲을 가로지르는 길을 표시하는 데 사용되었을지도 모르며, 광부들은 지하에 있는 그들의 작업장을 밝히는 데 반딧불이가 든 병을 사용해 왔다. 흔한 광원과는 달리, 생물 발광은 열을 거의 내지 않으므로 많은 상황에서 매력적인 도구이다.

　오늘날에는, 생물 발광을 훨씬 더 많이 적용할 수 있다. 예를 들어, 그것은 물속의 독성 물질을 경고하는 데 사용된다. 물속의 생물 발광 박테리아는 독성 물질이 있으면 더 흐릿해져서 살충제나 중금속으로부터의 오염이 있는지 검사하도록 사람들에게 경고한다. 또한, 발명가들은 자신들이 서식하는 물이 움직일 때 빛을 내는 조류를 이용해 친환경적인 램프를 만들기 위해 노력하고 있다. 이러한 램프는 에너지 사용량과 광공해를 줄여줄 것으로 기대된다. 의학 연구에서 반딧불이의 루시페라아제는 그것이 근적외선을 방출하게 하는 염료와 혼합되는데, 그 근적외선은 비교적 두꺼운 조직층을 통해 감지될 수 있다. 이 혼합물은 혈액 응고 단백질을 표시하는 데 사용되어 혈액 희석제의 효과를 추적 관찰하는 것을 더 용이하게 해 준다.

　생물 발광은 인류보다 더 오래되었지만, 현대 기술은 그것에 완전히 새로운 용도를 제공하고 있다. 한때는 불가사의한 현상이었던 것이 이제는 우리가 우리의 신체와 우리를 둘러싼 세계를 더 잘 이해하게 도와주고, 바라건대 우리가 최소한의 환경적인 영향을 주는 빛을 만들어 내는 방법들을 찾도록 해 주고 있다.

구문 해설

21행 In addition, inventors are trying to create eco-friendly lamps from algae {that glow when the water [(that[which]) they live in ∧] moves}.

23행 In medical research, firefly luciferase is mixed with a dye [that **causes** it **to emit** near-infrared light], *which* can be detected through ....
▶ cause + 목적어 + to-v: ~이 …하게 하다
▶ which는 near-infrared light를 선행사로 하는 계속적 용법의 관계대명사

25행 This mixture is used to mark blood clotting proteins, **making** it easier *to monitor* the effectiveness of blood thinners.
▶ making 이하는 결과를 나타내는 분사구문
▶ make + 목적어 + 형용사: ~을 …하게 만들다
▶ it은 가목적어, to monitor 이하가 진목적어

UNIT 12.
Social Issues

READING 1   p. 62~63

WORD FOCUS   contain

hold 담다 / include 포함하다 / comprise 포함하다 / carry 가지고 있다

WORD CHECK

1. employ   2. suffer   3. legitimate   4. component
5. extract

▶ endangered: being extremely threatened, especially due to limited population numbers

정답

1. d   2. c   3. d   4. d   5. They can refuse to buy any coltan coming from military groups. / They can work to support legitimate coltan mines, making sure the profits are used to benefit communities.   6. conflict, weapons, improve, recycle

해석

여러분은 주로 아프리카에서 발견되는 광물의 한 종류인 콜탄에 대해 한 번도 들어본 적이 없을지도 모른다. 하지만 이것은 아마 여러분의 인생에서 큰 부분을 차지하고 있을 희귀한 금속인 탄탈럼을 포함하고 있다. 탄탈럼은 카메라, 노트북, 휴대 전화의 필수 구성 요소인 탄탈럼 축전기를 만드는 데 사용된다. 이 점이 탄탈럼을 매우 가치 있게 만드는 것은 당연한 것이고, 사실 너무 귀하기 때문에 그것을 두고 심한 갈등이 빚어지고 있다.

전 세계 콜탄의 약 80%는 콩고 민주 공화국에서 발견된다. 현재 이 국가는 폭력적인 무력 분쟁을 겪고 있고, 대부분의 콜탄 광산은 군사 세력에 의해 통제된다. 그들은 콜탄을 추출하고 이웃 국가에 판매하여 그 돈을 더 많은 무기를 사는 데 사용한다.

점점 더 많은 사람들이 매년 탄탈럼을 함유한 전자 기기를 구매하고 있다. 이러한 수요를 충족시키기 위해서는 많은 양의 콜탄이 땅에서 채굴되어야 한다. 많은 경우에 어린 아이들이 광산에서 일하도록 강요당한다. 이 분쟁으로 농경지가 훼손된 많은 농부들도 이러한 광산에 고용된다. 비록 적정한 임금을 받고 있지만, 그들은 종종 무장 군인들에게 급료를 강탈당한다.

하지만 인간들만 부정적인 영향을 받고 있는 것은 아니다. 그 지역의 야생 동물들 또한 고통받고 있다. 멸종 위기에 처한 고릴라들이 콜탄이 채굴되는 지역에 서식하고 있고, 그들은 채굴 과정에서 자주 죽임을 당한다. 콩고의 동쪽 지역은 한때 동부 저지대 고릴라 수천 마리의 서식지였다. 현재 개체 수는 알려져 있지 않지만, 50% 이상 감소한 것으로 여겨진다.

콩고의 이 분쟁은 쉬운 해결책이 없는 복잡한 상황이다. 하지만 기업들이 군사 세력이 제공하는 콜탄을 구입하는 것을 거부함으로써 이 상황을 개선할 수 있다. 게다가, 콩고 내에서는 (콜탄 채굴로부터의) 수익이 반드시

지역 사회에 이득이 되는 데 쓰이도록 하면서 기업들은 적법한 콜탄 광산을 지원하기 위해 노력할 수 있다.

개개인도 도움을 줄 수 있다. 매년 새로운 것을 사는 대신, 가지고 있던 전자 기기를 유지하며 콜탄의 수요를 줄일 수 있다. 그리고 새로운 모델로 업그레이드를 할 때 오래된 물건을 쓰레기통에 버리는 대신 재활용하거나 자선 단체에 기증할 수도 있다. 아주 작은 노력이라도 수백만 명의 소비자들에 의해 행해지면 변화를 일으킬 수 있다.

구문 해설

[6행] ... **so** valuable, in fact, **that** a terrible conflict is being fought over it.
     ▶ so ~ that ...: 너무 ~해서 …하다

[14행] Many farmers, **whose** fields have been destroyed in
    <u>   </u>
    _S
    the fighting, <u>are also employed</u> by these mines.
                    _V
     ▶ whose는 계속적 용법의 관계대명사

[29행] Even the smallest efforts, when (**they are**) made by millions of consumers, can make a difference.
     ▶ 부사절의 주어가 주절의 주어와 같은 경우 「부사절의 주어 + be 동사」는 생략 가능

READING 2   p. 64~65

WORD FOCUS   ethnic

ethnic difference 민족적 차이 / ethnic group 인종 집단 / ethnic identity 민족 정체성 / ethnic minority 소수 민족

WORD CHECK

1. embrace   2. demographics   3. immigrate
4. multiracial   5. diverse

▶ encourage: to support and promote sth, such as an idea or an opinion

정답

1. a   2. b   3. (A) immigrants (B) the Canadian government   4. (1) F (2) O (3) F (4) O   5. d
6. population, transnational, accepted, model

해석

수십 년 전에는 한국에서 외국인을 거의 보기 힘들었고, 많은 한국인들은 자신의 나라가 인종적 다양성이 거의 없다는 사실에 실제로 자부심을 느꼈다. 하지만 상황이 확실히 변했다. 한국이 세계화함에 따라, 한국의 인구도 민족적, 인종적으로 더 다양해지기 시작하고 있다.

이 변화는 한국 전쟁 후에 일어났는데, 그때는 한국이 재건하고 외세를 받아들이기 시작한 때였다. 한국은 몇십 년간 급격히 성장했고 사업과 기술 분야에서 강대국으로서의 입지를 다졌다. 많은 외국인들이 일하기 위해 한국에 오기 시작했는데, 그것은 점차적으로 한국의 인구 통계를 넓혔

다. 그러는 동안, 많은 한국 가구들은 다국적 결혼을 통해 다른 배경 출신의 사람들을 맞이했다.

안타깝게도, 이러한 다인종 가구의 구성원들은 한국에 이민 온 사람들 중 다수와 마찬가지로, (한국에) 받아들여졌다고 느끼기가 항상 쉽지는 않다. 일부 한국인은 아직도 다른 문화권 출신의 사람들을 한국인으로 여기는 것을 어려워한다. 이런 낡은 태도를 바꾸고 모두가 조화를 이루며 살 방법을 찾을 필요가 있다.

한국에 모범을 보여줄 수 있는 한 나라가 캐나다이다. 캐나다는 세계에서 이민자 비율이 가장 높으며, 다문화주의를 국가의 공식 정책으로 삼은 최초의 나라였다. 이민자들이 캐나다의 문화를 받아들이기를 기대하기보다, 캐나다 정부는 이민자들이 자신의 고유한 문화와 정체성을 유지하도록 장려한다. 동시에 그들은 이민자들이 캐나다를 새로운 조국으로 받아들이고 캐나다 사회를 존중할 것을 기대한다.

국경을 통해 다수의 이민자를 허용한다고 해서 자동으로 다문화 국가가 되는 것은 아니다. 새로 온 사람들의 문화와 신념을 진정으로 이해하고 받아들이는 것이 필요하다. 이 과정은 수년이 걸릴 수도 있는데, 기성세대의 태도를 바꾸는 것은 대개 꽤 어렵기 때문이다. 그러나 이곳이 현재 한국이 서 있는 자리이며, 다문화주의로 가는 여정의 첫발을 내딛고 있는 것이다.

구문 해설

13행 Unfortunately, members of these multiracial [S] families, along with many of the people who have immigrated to Korea, do not always **find** it **easy** to [V] *feel* accepted.
- ▶ find + 목적어 + 형용사: ~을 …하다고 여기다
- ▶ it은 가목적어, to feel 이하가 진목적어

14행 Some Koreans still **have a hard time** *thinking of* people from other cultures *as* being Korean.
- ▶ have a hard time v-ing: ~하는 데 어려움을 겪다
- ▶ think of A as B: A를 B로 생각하다[여기다]

19행 **Rather than** expecting immigrants to adopt Canadian culture, ...
- ▶ rather than: ~하기보다는, ~ 대신에

26행 Yet this is (the place) **where** Korea now finds itself, ...
- ▶ 관계부사 where 앞에는 선행사 the place가 생략됨

WORD REVIEW TEST

1. b   2. d   3. c   4. c   5. b   6. a   7. d   8. c
9. a   10. b   11. spoiled   12. replaceable
13. flexible   14. metabolism   15. minimal

1. a   2. d   3. c   4. a   5. c   6. b   7. a
8. immigrated   9. destroyed   10. Ethnic
11. endangered   12. adopt   13. charity
14. border   15. armed

UNIT 13.
Psychology

WORD FOCUS   academic

academic career 학력 / academic success 학문적 성공 / academic writing 학술적 글쓰기 / purely academic 순전히 학문적인

WORD CHECK

1. esteem   2. extensive   3. requirement
4. potential   5. hierarchy
▶ vocation: a career considered to be a lifelong choice

정답

1. b   2. (1) ⓑ (2) ⓒ (3) ⓐ   3. b   4. Its concept is vague and there's no evidence to show that every individual can reach it.   5. (1) T (2) T (3) F   6. basic, potential, recognition, problems

해석

삶의 기본적인 필요조건은 무엇이고 그다음에는 무엇이 필요할까? 여러분이 이 질문들에 답을 한다면 미국의 심리학자 에이브럼 매슬로가 그의 '욕구 단계설'에서 행한 것과 같은 작업을 하고 있는 것이다. 그 이론에서 말하는 바는 우리가 여러 단계를 거쳐 나아가야 하는데, 각 단계의 욕구를 충족시키고 난 다음에야 다음 단계로 옮겨갈 수 있다는 것이다. 매슬로는 개개인이 몇몇 기본적인 욕구들을 충족시킬 수 있다면 결국에는 자신이 지닌 잠재력을 실현시킬 수 있을 것이라고 생각했다.

가장 기본적인 욕구들은 매슬로의 단계설의 최하부를 형성하며 생리적 욕구라고 불린다. 생리적 욕구는 음식과 주거지에 대한 우리의 욕구를 포함한다. 이런 것들이 충족되지 않으면, 우리는 다음 단계인 안전에 대한 욕구로 옮겨가지 못한다. 우리는 처한 환경에서 안전함을 느끼고자 하는데, 이런 안전함은 대개 보호와, 두려움으로부터의 자유를 의미한다. 제3단계는 애정과 소속에 대한 욕구이다. 사람들은 단체에 가입하거나 그것을 만들고, 친구를 사귀고, 팀의 일원이 됨으로써뿐만 아니라 가족과 가정을 통해서도 이 욕구를 충족시킨다.

제4단계인 존중에 대한 욕구는 인정받고자 하는 사람의 욕구를 말한다. 이 단계에서 사람들은 다른 사람들이 자신을 높이 평가한다고 여기고 싶어 한다. 그들은 칭찬을 필요로 하고 자기 자신에 대해 만족하고 싶어 하기도 한다. 사람들은 정해진 목표를 달성함으로써 이를 얻기 위해 노력하기도 한다. 제5단계인 자아실현 욕구는 매슬로의 욕구 단계설의 정점에 해당한다. 이는 인간의 최대 잠재력에 도달하려는 추구이다. 이 과정에서 사람들은 진실, 정의, 지혜, 정신적인 충만함과 같은 욕구를 갖게 되는 경향이 있다.

매슬로의 단계설이 지닌 흥미로운 논리에도 불구하고, 거기에는 몇 가지 한계가 있는 것으로 보인다. 단계를 서열화하는 것과 분명한 단계가 있다는 주장에 대한 증거가 미비하다는 것이 광범위한 연구를 통해 제기되어 왔다. 게다가 자아실현 욕구라는 개념이 모호하며, 개개인 모두가 그것에 도달할 수 있다는 것을 보여주는 증거도 전혀 없다.

매슬로는 인간의 욕구에 대한 학문적 연구를 수행한 최초의 심리학자였다. 그는 모든 사람이 삶에서 자신의 천직을 발견하고 더 나은 삶을 위해 노력하도록 장려되어야 한다고 생각했다. 이는 오늘날에도 여전히 귀중한 교훈이다.

구문 해설

[3행] ..., you're doing the same kind of work [that American psychologist Abraham Maslow did ∧ in his ...].

[13행] People satisfy this need *through their families and homes*, **as well as** *by joining and forming groups, making friends, and being part of a team.*
▶ A as well as B: 'B뿐만 아니라 A도'라는 뜻으로, 위 문장의 as well as는 through와 by가 이끄는 두 개의 전치사구를 연결함

READING 2   p. 70~71

WORD FOCUS particular

specific 특정한 / certain 특정한, 일정한 / distinct 별개의 / special 특수한

WORD CHECK

1. regulate   2. stimulate   3. fascinating   4. inherit
5. isolate
▶ consistent: staying the same over a period of time

정답

1. a   2. c   3. b   4. Perhaps it is regulated less than usual and some information moves backwards.
5. stimulates, letters, connections, information

해석

1965년도의 노벨 물리학상 수상자인 리처드 파인만은 자신이 글자들을 특정한 색으로 본다고 말했다. 예를 들어, 그는 J라는 글자를 연한 황갈색으로, N이라는 글자를 남보라색으로, 그리고 X라는 글자를 짙은 갈색으로 보았다. 그가 묘사한 그 경험은 두 가지 다른 유형의 감각적 인식 사이의 일관적인 연결인 공감각으로 알려져 있다.

'공감각'이라는 단어는 '함께'와 '느낌'을 의미하는 그리스어 어근으로부터 형성되었다. 일반적으로 오감은 서로 분리되어 있지만, 공감각은 한 감각이나, 특정한 유형의 지각으로부터의 입력이 또 다른 것도 자극할 때 생긴다. 그것은 시각, 청각, 촉각, 미각, 후각에 관한 경험들의 어떤 결합도 포함할 수 있다. 가장 흔한 유형 중 하나는 리처드 파인만이 서술한 경험과 같이 색을 글자, 숫자, 혹은 모양과 연관시키는 것이다. 또 다른 유형은 색을 소리와 연관시키는 것이다. 이것의 유명한 예는 작곡가인 프란츠 리스트에게서 비롯되는데, 그는 자신의 관현악단에게 '조금 더 파랗게'나 '너무 장미 같지 않도록!' 연주하라고 말하곤 했다.

연구는 공감각을 지닌 사람들이 보통 그것을 가지고 태어나거나 유아기에 그것을 발달시킨다는 것과, 그것이 유전적으로 전해질 수 있다는 것을 보여주었다. 연구자들은 또한 사람들에게 오랜 기간을 두고 떨어져 있는 시점에서 그들의 공감각적 연상을 말해 달라고 요청했고, 그것들이 매우 유사하다는 것을 알아냈다. 예를 들어, 한 여성은 그녀가 100개의 다른 단어들과 연관시킨 색을 나열해 달라는 요청을 받았다. 일 년 후에, 예고 없이 그녀는 동일한 것을 요청받았는데 그 단어들 중 90개가 넘는 것에 같은 대답을 했다.

사람들이 공감각을 경험할 때 뇌에서 정확히 무슨 일이 일어나는지에 관한 다양한 이론이 있다. 어떤 연구자들은 감각을 다루는 뇌의 영역들이 단순히 평소보다 그것들 사이에 더 많은 연결망을 가진다고 생각한다. 다른 연구자들은 정보는 보통 신경 연결망을 따라 특정 방향으로 흘러간다고 지적한다. 공감각은 아마 이 흐름이 평소보다 덜 통제되어 일부 정보가 '뒤로' 이동할 때 발생하는 것일지도 모른다.

뇌 연구에 있어서의 우리의 모든 진보에도, 우리는 아직 공감각에 대해 연구할 것이 많다. 유전학 연구와, 활동 중인 뇌를 보여주는 영상 기술을 통해, 연구자들은 더 많이 알게 되기를 바란다. 현재로서는, 공감각의 수수께끼는 그저 그것을 흥미롭게 만들어주는 것의 일부이다.

구문 해설

[16행] Studies have shown ⌐ that people ... childhood
                              | and
                              └ that it can be inherited ....

[17행] Researchers have also **asked** people **to describe** their synesthetic associations at points [separated by long periods of time] ....
▶ ask + 목적어 + to-v: ~에게 …해 달라고 요청하다

[24행] Some researchers think {**that** areas of the brain [**that** deal with the senses] simply have ...}.
▶ 첫 번째 that은 접속사, 두 번째 that은 주격 관계대명사

UNIT 14.
Environment

WORD CHECK

1. vegetation   2. declare   3. reproduce
4. ecosystem   5. habitat
▶ vehicle: sth that carries or transports sth else

정답

1. c   2. It has led to a dramatic decline in elephant populations over the past few decades.   3. d   4. b
5. They are too small and too isolated from each other to allow elephant populations to recover.   6. b
7. (1) ⓒ (2) ⓑ (3) ⓓ (4) ⓐ

해석

　　인간의 행동이 계속해서 코끼리들의 자연환경에 영향을 끼치게 되면서 코끼리들은 점점 더 위협에 직면하고 있다. 1900년 이후 아시아와 아프리카에 거주하는 사람들의 수가 4배 증가하였는데, 이것은 코끼리들이 그들의 서식지 중 일부를 인간의 정착지에 빼앗겨왔음을 의미한다. 1990년에 상아의 판매가 금지되긴 했지만, 그것에 대한 수요는 오늘날까지도 계속된다. 이것은 지난 몇십 년에 걸쳐 코끼리의 개체 수를 급격하게 감소시켜 왔다. 수치들은 1930년 이후로 아프리카코끼리의 개체 수가 90%넘게 감소하여, 6백만 마리가 넘었던 것이 현재는 5십만 마리도 채 되지 않음을 보여준다. 아시아코끼리는 그보다도 훨씬 더 적게 남아서 겨우 3만 5천에서 4만 마리만이 여전히 존재한다.

　　코끼리가 생태계에서 수행하는 중대한 역할을 고려할 때, 코끼리 멸종의 위험은 걱정스러운 일이다. 거대하고 막강한 소비자로서, 코끼리들은 그들의 환경에서 중추가 되는 종(種)이며 그들의 지역 서식지에 있는 생물의 다양성에 영향을 미친다. 그들은 대량의 목초를 먹어 치워서 많은 토지를 개간하는 것의 원인이 되고, 초원의 생성과 보존에 기여하게 된다. 이 초원은 영양과 같은 다른 동물들에게 서식지를 제공한다.

　　게다가, 코끼리의 배설물도 자연환경에 중요한 역할을 한다. 개코원숭이와 새들은 코끼리 배설물을 들춰 소화되지 않은 씨앗이나 나무 열매를 찾고, 쇠똥구리는 이 퇴적물 안에서 번식 활동을 한다. 영양가가 풍부한 그 배설물은 또한 손상된 토양이 회복되는 데 도움을 주기도 한다. 마지막으로, 이 배설물은 광대한 지역에 걸쳐 씨앗을 퍼뜨리는 매개체가 된다. 몇몇 씨앗들이 코끼리의 소화계를 통과하지 않고서는 자라지 못할 것이라는 사실을 아는 것은 중요하다.

　　코끼리를 구하고자 하는 노력의 일환으로, 환경보호 단체들은 코끼리들을 멸종 위기에 처한 종(種)으로 공표했으며, 그들을 사냥꾼들로부터 보호하기 위해 드론과 GPS 기술을 이용해오고 있다. 또한, 많은 코끼리 서식지가 국립 공원으로 보존되어 왔다. 그러나 대부분의 환경 운동가들은 이 공원

들이 코끼리의 개체 수를 회복시키기에는 너무나 작고 서로 너무 떨어져 있다고 생각한다. 대부분의 사람들이 확실히 동의하는 부분은 진지한 국제 협력이 없다면 코끼리들은 가까운 미래에 멸종될 위험에 직면한다는 것이다.

구문 해설

[10행] There are **even** fewer Asian elephants left; ....
▶ even은 비교급을 강조하는 부사

[11행] The threat of elephant extinction is worrisome **in view of** the vital role [(that[which]) they play ∧ in the ecosystem].
▶ in view of: ~을 고려하여, ~의 점에서 보아

[25행] ... the parks are **too** small and **too** isolated from each other **to** ***allow*** elephant populations *to recover*.
▶ too ~ to-v: …하기에 너무 ~하다
▶ allow + 목적어 + to-v: ~이 …하도록 해 주다

[26행] What most people **do** agree on is that without
              S   V   C
serious international cooperation, ...
▶ 동사의 의미를 강조하기 위해 동사 agree 앞에 조동사 do가 쓰임

WORD FOCUS   indicator

sign 표시 / signal 신호 / gauge 측정 기준 / index 지표

WORD CHECK

1. conservation   2. destination   3. designate
4. vast   5. delicate
▶ toxic: containing poisonous chemicals

정답

1. a   2. They absorb carbon dioxide as they build their shells.   3. ⓒ   4. b   5. (1) F (2) T (3) F (4) T
6. (1) ⓒ (2) ⓑ (3) ⓔ (4) ⓐ (5) ⓓ

해석

　　수 세기 동안 사람들은 몇몇 인상적인 구조물들을 만들어 왔지만, 여러분은 어떤 생물군에 의해 만들어진, 가장 커다란 알려진 구조물이 호주 연안의 그레이트 배리어 리프라는 것을 알았는가? 이 거대한 암초 체계는 344,400 평방 킬로미터에 걸쳐져 있고 2,900개의 개별 암초로 나뉠 수 있는데, 모두 자신의 주변에 딱딱한 껍질을 형성하고 있는 작은 산호충에 의해 만들어진 것이다. 그 암초는 1981년에 세계 문화유산으로 지정되었으며, 그것은 다양한 야생 생물 군집을 서식하게 해 주고 지구의 건강을 나타내는 중요한 지표 역할을 한다.

　　그레이트 배리어 리프는 400종류의 산호와 1,500종의 어류를 포함하는 엄청나게 많은 종의 서식지이며, 듀공과 바다거북 같은 멸종 위기에 처

한 종에게 살 곳을 제공해 준다. 산호충은 껍질을 형성할 때 이산화탄소를 흡수하기 때문에, 그 암초 체계는 세계의 기후를 조절하는 데 도움이 된다. 암초 체계는 또한 큰 파도와 거친 날씨를 호주 해안으로부터 몰아내어 그곳을 사람들이 살기에 더 안전한 곳으로 만들어 준다.

현재, 그 암초는 자신의 건강과, 심지어 생존에 있어서도 몇 가지 위험에 직면해 있다. 그곳은 인기 있는 관광지인데, 부주의한 방문객들이 그곳을 훼손하고 있다. 육지에서의 사람들의 행위도 그 암초를 위협하고 있는데, 비료와 농약이 물에 씻겨 들어가서 그곳을 일부 생물에게 유독하게 만들기 때문이다. 그러나 가장 심각한 것은 기후 변화로 인해 초래되는 위험이다. 산호는 특정 수온 범위 내에서 가장 건강하기 때문에 더 따뜻한 물은 그것을 질병과 죽음의 위험에 처하게 하는데, 이는 결국 산호에 의존하는 전체 생태계를 위태롭게 한다.

암초를 보호하기 위해, 호주인들은 보호 프로그램과, 관광객을 위한 지침서를 만들었다. 정부와 민간 자금 모두가 암초 주변의 수질을 향상하고, 그것의 건강에 대한 특정 위협에 대처하는 데 사용되고 있다. 암초를 방문하는 관광객들은 그 지역을 훼손하지 않도록 호주 에코투어리즘 협회에 의해 인증된 여행 옵션을 선택함으로써 보호 노력에 기여할 수 있다.

수년간, 사람들은 그레이트 배리어 리프를 주로 관광지로 생각해 왔다. 그곳은 또한 생물학자와 자연을 사랑하는 사람들에게 아주 멋진 곳이기도 하다. 하지만 우리가 그곳을 그밖에 다른 곳으로 보기 전에, 우리는 그곳이 쉽게 다칠 수 있으며 보호받아야 하는 연약한 생물들이 모여있는 곳이라는 것을 기억해야 한다.

구문 해설

13행
It also keeps large waves and rough weather away from the coast of Australia, **making** it a safer place **for people** *to live*.

▶ making 이하는 결과를 나타내는 분사구문
▶ to live는 a safer place를 수식하는 형용사적 용법의 to부정사이며, for people은 to live의 의미상의 주어

27행
However, before we **view** it **as** anything else, we need to remember {*that* it is a collection of delicate living things [*that* can easily be injured and ...]}.

▶ view A as B: A를 B로 바라보다[여기다]
▶ 첫 번째 that은 접속사, 두 번째 that은 주격 관계대명사

WORD REVIEW TEST

1. b 2. d 3. c 4. b 5. a 6. c 7. b
8. endeavor 9. composer 10. associates
11. inherited 12. fulfill 13. evidence
14. involve 15. neural 16. physiological

---

1. c 2. d 3. b 4. a 5. c 6. d 7. a 8. b
9. reproduce 10. endangered 11. contributes
12. maintenance 13. ban 14. threaten
15. settlement

UNIT 15.
Politics

READING 1   p. 78~79

WORD FOCUS common

common approach 일반적인 방법 / common sense 상식 /
common error 흔한 실수 / fairly common 상당히 흔한

WORD CHECK

1. eligible 2. inhabitant 3. profound 4. stability
5. outnumber

▶ executive: being related to the responsibility of making and carrying out laws and decisions

정답

1. c 2. b 3. c 4. Because Spartan society suffered from a fear of a slave rebellion and it wanted to retain stability. 5. Because only a small percentage of men had influence, women could not vote, and slaves did most of the work. 6. government, executive, military, limited

해석

기원전 6세기에는 고대 그리스에서 경쟁 관계의 도시 국가들이 서로 권력 쟁탈을 벌임에 따라 급속한 변화가 전개되었다. 이 도시 국가들 중 가장 강력한 두 국가였던 아테네와 스파르타는 각각 고대 그리스의 미래에 깊은 영향을 끼칠 독특한 특성을 가진 서로 다른 정부 체제를 발전시켰다.

아테네는 '시민'에 의해 통치되는 민주주의의 도입으로 황금기를 맞았다. 불레(Boule)라고 알려져 있는 평의회가 집행권과 행정권 모두를 가졌다. 이 평의회의 의원들은 선거가 아니라 추첨으로 선정되었으며, 재임 기간은 1년이었다. 30세 이상의 어떤 시민도 자격이 있었지만, 아테네에서 태어난 남자들만이 시민으로 간주되었다. 모든 시민들에게 개방이 된 의회는 법을 통과시키고 정책을 결정했다.

한편, 스파르타에서는 과두 정치가 발달했는데, 그곳은 두 최고 귀족 집안 출신의 두 명의 왕과 에포르(Ephor)라고 알려져 있는 5명의 유력한 지도자들에 의해 통치되었으며, 이 지도자들은 스파르타의 왕들을 통제할 특

권과 함께 행정과 집행에 대한 전권을 가졌다. 이 에포르들은 차례로 스파르티아트에 의해 선출되었는데, 그들은 사회의 최상위층을 형성하며 전적인 법적·정치적 권리를 부여받은 유일한 주민들인 30세 이상의 남성 스파르타 토착민이었다.

그것들의 뚜렷한 긍정적인 특성에도 불구하고, 이 두 도시 국가들은 그들의 체제에 한계점이 있었다. 스파르타에서는 노예가 그들의 주인에 비해 7대 1 정도로 많았으며, 그 도시는 노예가 된 사람들의 노동 없이는 기능할 수 없었다. 따라서 스파르타 사회는 노예 반란에 대한 두려움으로 고통받았고, 안정을 유지하기 위해 군사 국가를 발전시켰다. 스파르타와 대조적으로, 아테네에서는 민주주의가 수립될 수 있었다. 하지만 그것은 제한된 민주주의였는데, 그 안에서는 소수의 남자들만 영향력을 가졌고, 여자들은 투표하지 못했으며, 노예들이 대부분의 노동을 했다.

구문 해설

1행

The 6th century B.C. witnessed [the development of
S   V
rapid changes in ancient Greece] ....

▶ 무생물 주어(The 6th century B.C.)를 의인화한 표현으로 '기원전 6세기에 ~(라는 사건)이 일어났다'라는 식으로 해석

14행

Meanwhile, an oligarchy had developed in Sparta, **which** was ruled by two kings ... and (by) a group of five powerful leaders known as Ephors, *who* had ....

▶ which는 Sparta를 선행사로 하는 계속적 용법의 관계대명사

▶ who는 계속적 용법의 관계대명사 (= and they)

READING 2 — TOEFL — p. 80~81

정답

1. ⓑ 2. ⓓ 3. the second square 4. ⓓ 5. ⓒ
6. ⓑ, ⓓ, ⓔ

해석

플라톤의 〈국가론〉

고대 아테네는 최초의 민주주의의 발원지였으며, 몇몇의 위대한 사상가들을 배출했다. 민주주의가 실패하기 시작하자, 그 당시의 철학자들은 그 이유를 알아내고 그것을 고칠 방법을 생각해 내려고 노력했다. 이러한 철학자들 중 한 사람이 소크라테스(기원전 469-399)의 제자인 플라톤(기원전 427-347)이었다. 플라톤은 그 시대의 민주주의에 의구심을 갖기 시작했고, 더 나은 대안을 생각해 내려고 했다.

그의 가장 유명한 저서 중 하나인 〈국가론〉에서 플라톤은 그의 이상 사회를 제안했다. 그것은 그가 국가가 지녀야 할 네 가지 덕목으로 본 것들, 즉 지혜, 용기, 절제, 그리고 정의에 기초를 두었다. 그는 이 덕목 중 세 개를 실현할 각기 다른 계급의 사람들을 지명했다. 지혜로운 사람들은 '철인 왕'으로서 통치하고, 용감한 사람들은 '수호자'로서 활동하고, 절제력이 있는 사람들은 '육체 노동'을 하여, 사회 전체가 정의를 향해 함께 협력해 나갈 것이라는 생각이었다.

플라톤은 인간의 영혼 때문에 그들이 천성적으로 이 역할들 중 한 가지를 수행하는 경향이 있다고 보았다. 플라톤에 의하면, 이 영혼은 세 개의 부분, 즉 이성, 의지, 그리고 욕구로 나뉜다. 만약 개인이 이성적인 요소에 의해 더 많이 지배를 받으면, 그 사람은 통치하는 데 적합하다. 의지에 의해 지배받는 사람은 좋은 수호자가 될 것이고, 욕구에 의해 지배받는 사람은 좋은 노동자가 될 것이다.

플라톤에게 있어서 사회의 궁극적인 목적은 욕구와 행복의 실현이었다. 모든 사람은 욕구를 가지며, 모든 사람은 능력을 가지고 있다. 하지만 사람들은 그들 개개인의 모든 욕구를 충족시키는 데 필요한 범위의 능력은 가지고 있지 않다. 따라서 그는 사회가 모든 사람들의 욕구를 만족시키기 위해서 함께 협력해야 한다고 생각했다. 모든 사람이 그들이 맡은 일을 전문으로 하고, 그들의 노동의 결실을 다른 사람들과 교환할 때, 모든 사람들은 그들의 욕구를 충족시키고 행복해질 수 있다. 결정적으로, 플라톤은 사회 구성 단위의 성공의 핵심 요소는 바로 왕들이 의사 결정을 하는 데 필요한 지혜이기 때문에, 완벽한 사회는 오직 왕이 철학자가 되거나 철학자가 왕이 될 때만 가능하다고 생각했다.

플라톤의 〈국가론〉은 사람들 속에 내재한 특질을 다루는 체제를 실행하기 위해 쓰여졌다. 이 책의 목표가 너무 비현실적이라서 실현될 수 없을 것 같긴 하지만, 그의 사상은 서양 철학의 토대를 마련했다.

구문 해설

2행

..., the philosophers of the time **tried to figure** out why **and (tried) to think** of ways to fix it.

9행

The wise would ..., **the brave** would ..., **the self-disciplined** would ....

▶ the + 형용사: ~한 사람들

22행

..., as **it** is the wisdom of their decision-making **that** is the key to the success of a social unit.

▶ it ~ that ... 강조구문으로, 주어인 the wisdom of their decision-making을 강조함

24행

Plato's *Republic* was designed to **put in place** a
system [that addressed the innate characteristics of the people].

▶ put + 목적어 + in place: ~을 실행하다

WORD REVIEW TEST

UNIT 15 — p. 82

1. b 2. a 3. d 4. c 5. a 6. b 7. d 8. b
9. a 10. d 11. c 12. ideal 13. lot
14. administrative

READING
EXPERT